Published by
Nature Photobook Publishing

The following 40 photographs have been specially selected to promote peace and tranquility.

Chosen from around the world, enjoy natural landscapes such as:
- Forests
- Beaches
- Waterfalls
- Lakes
- And more!

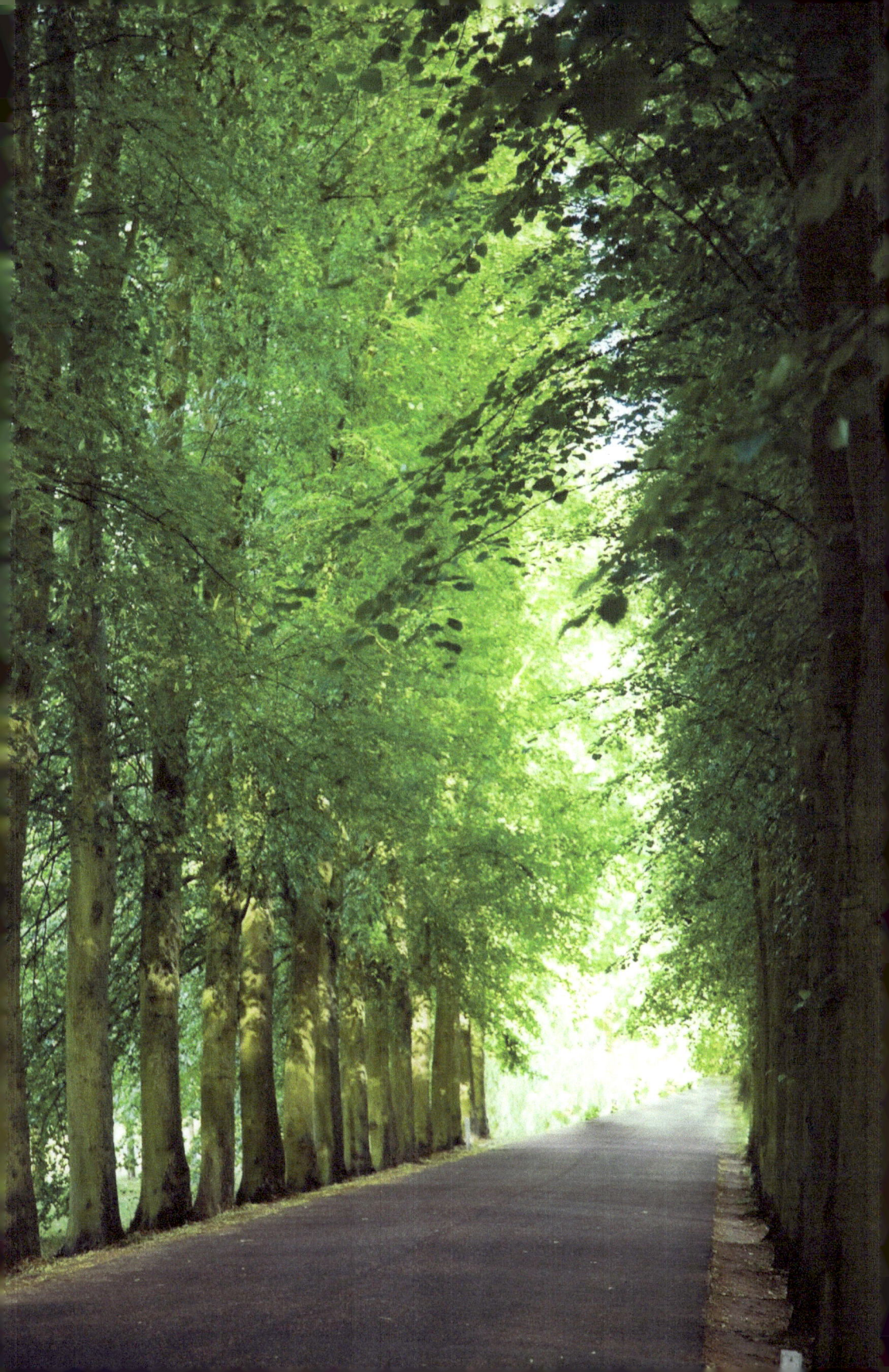

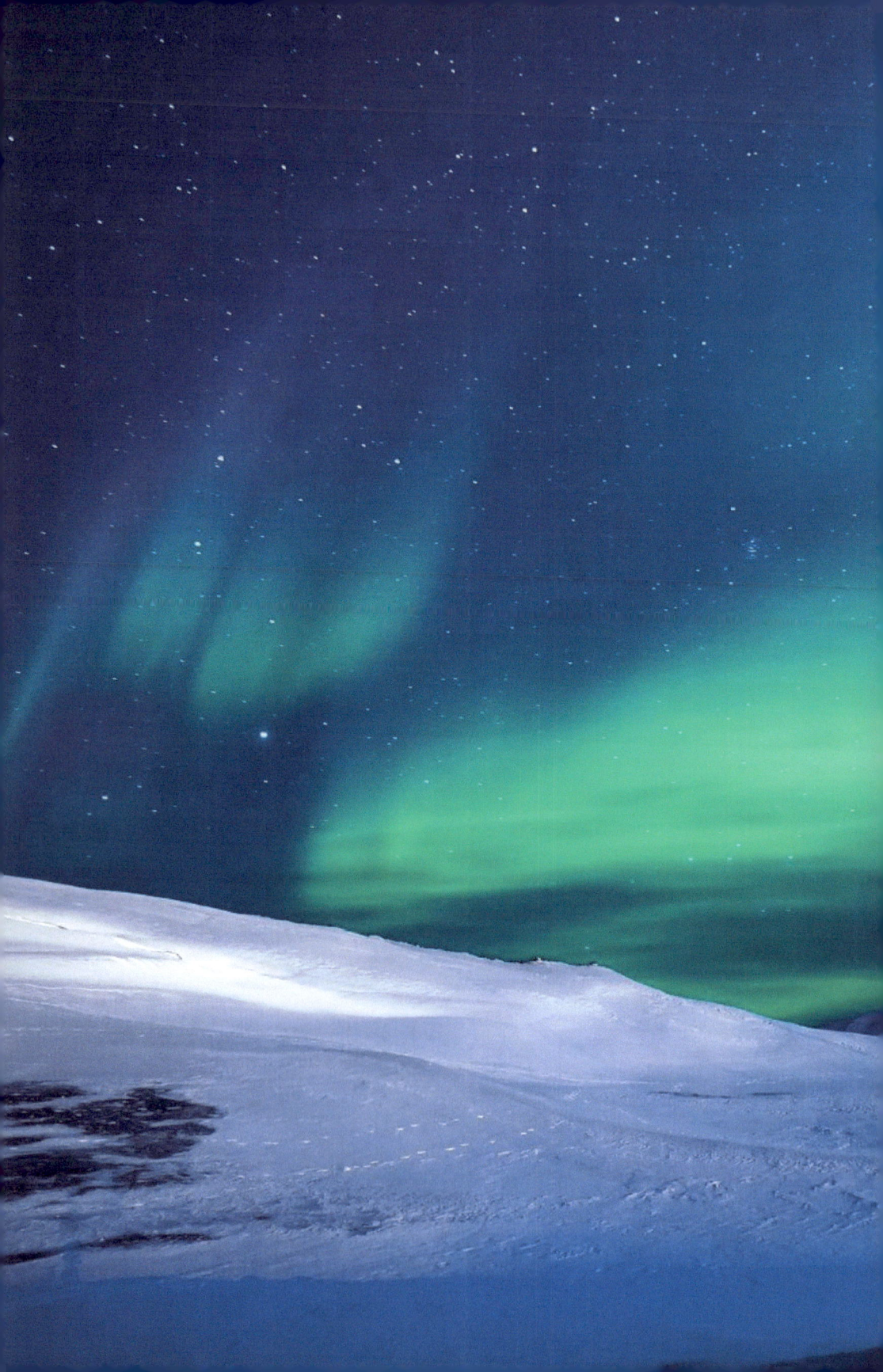

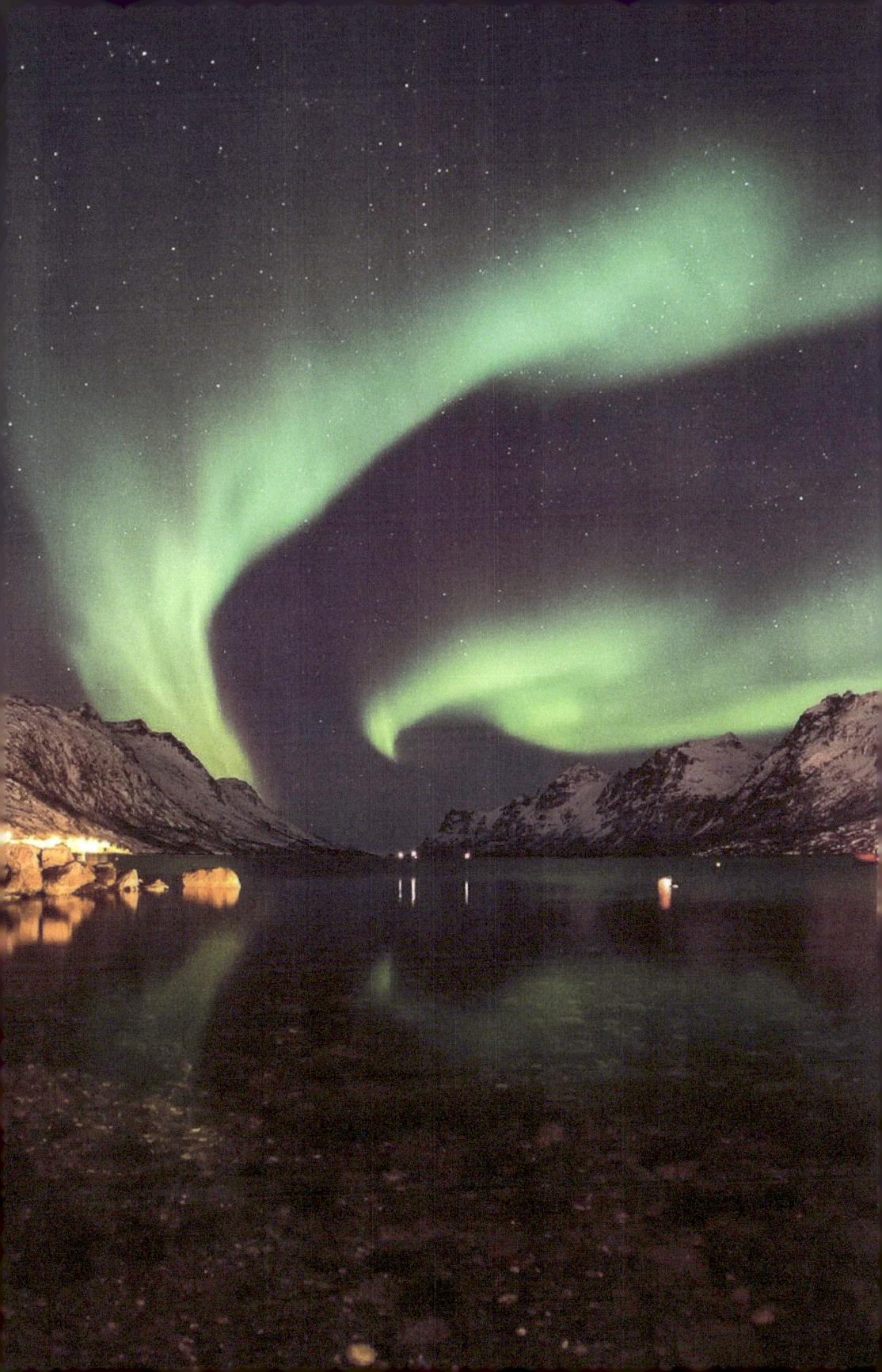

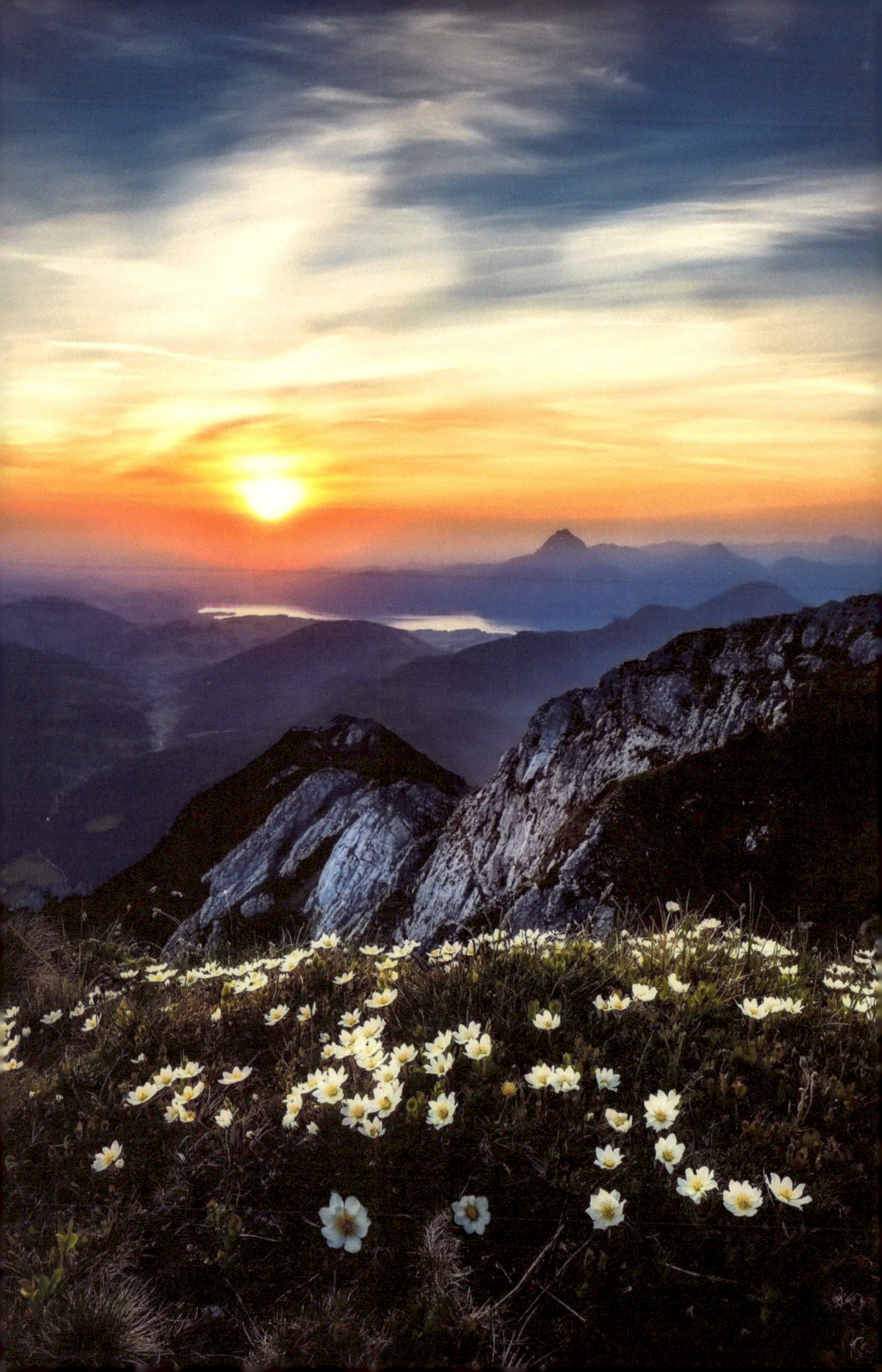

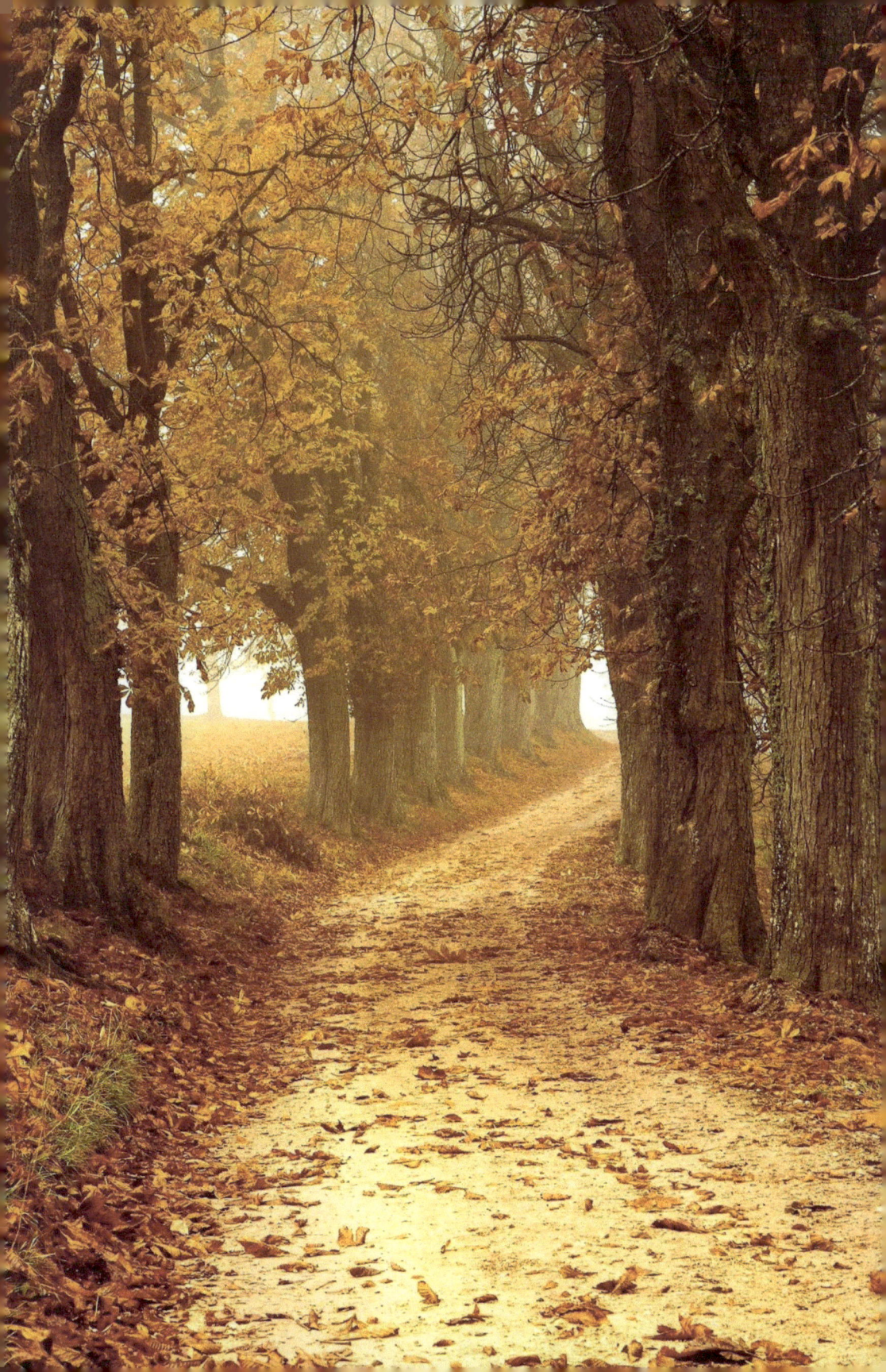

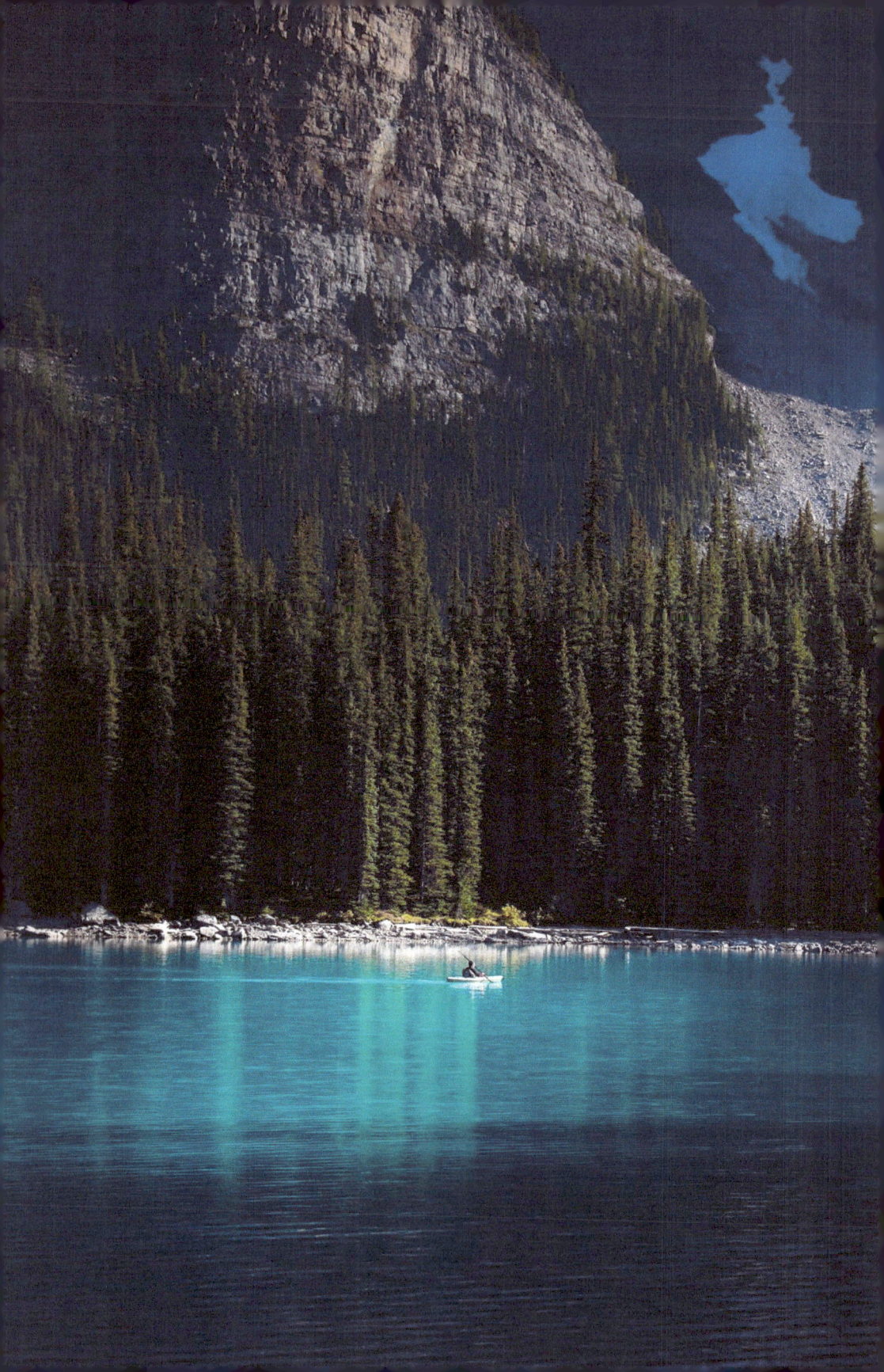

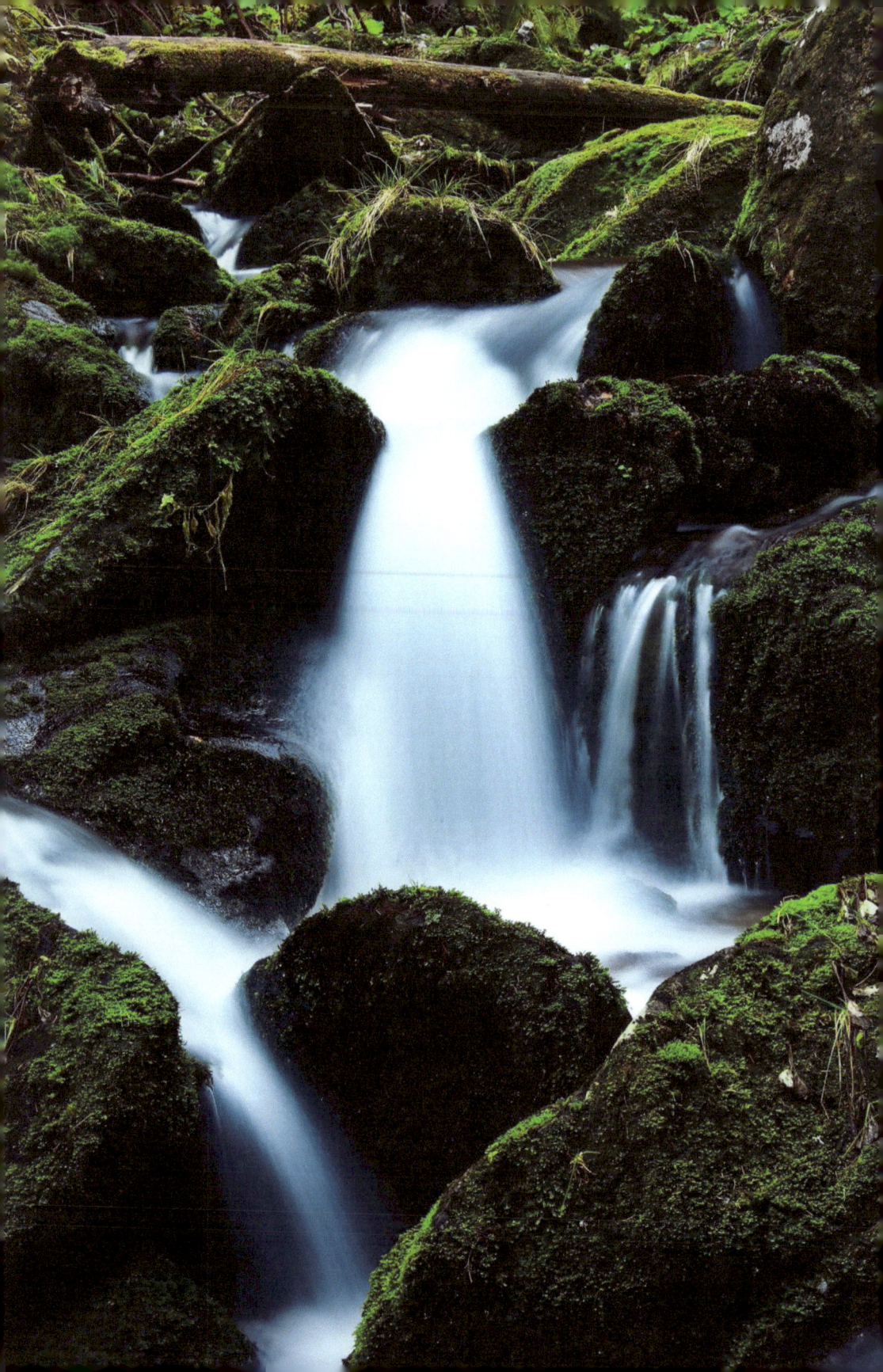

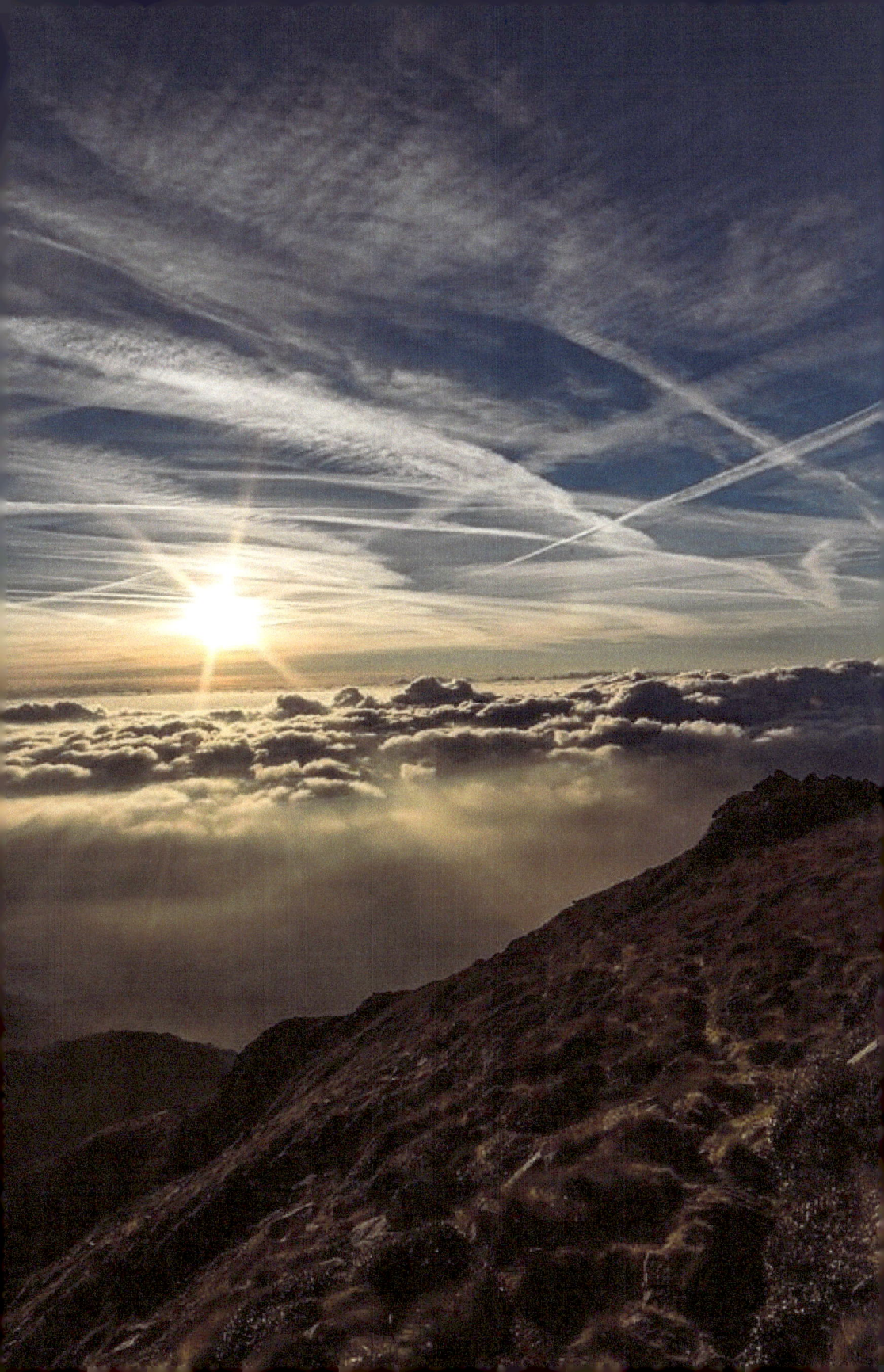

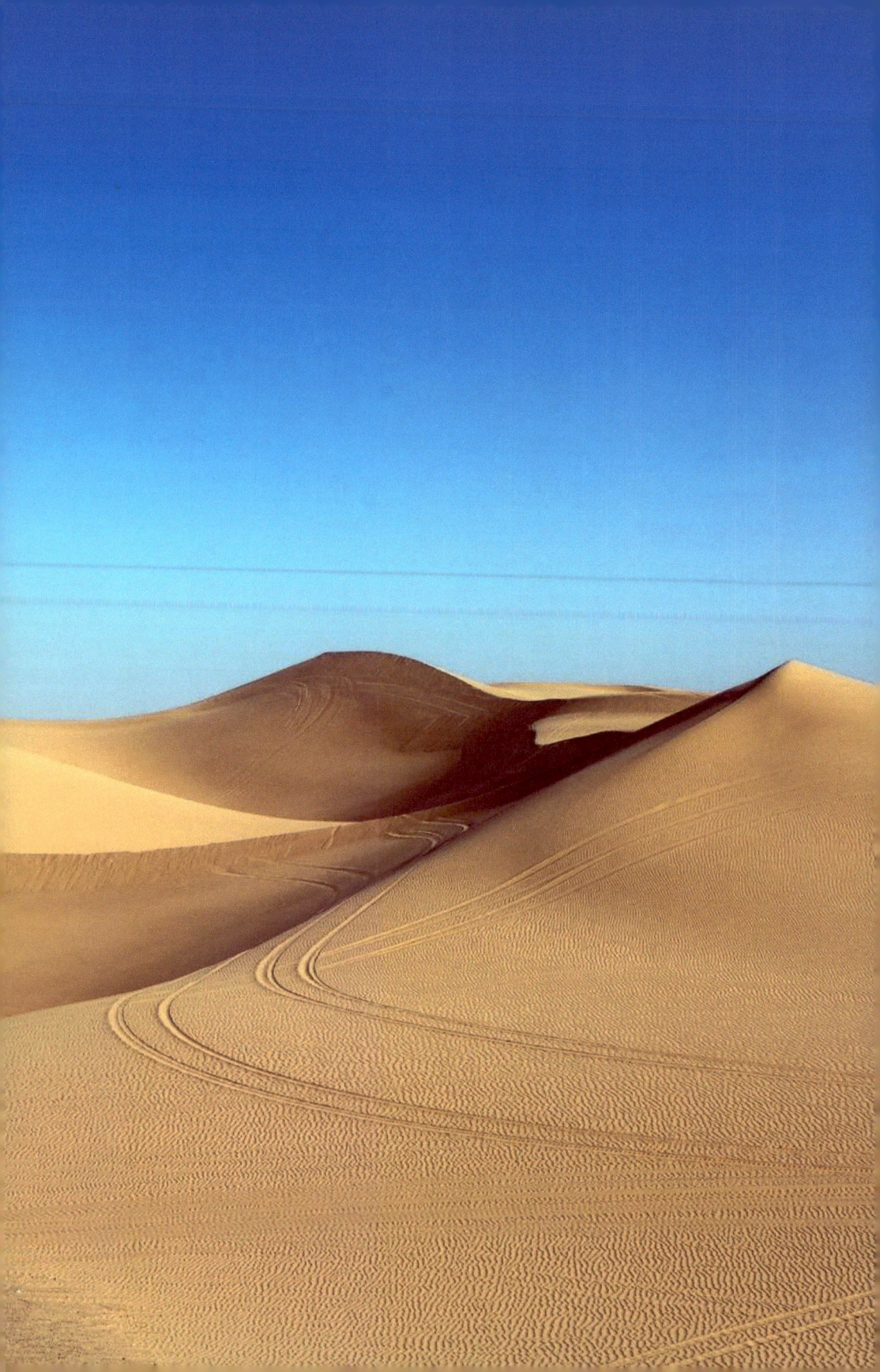

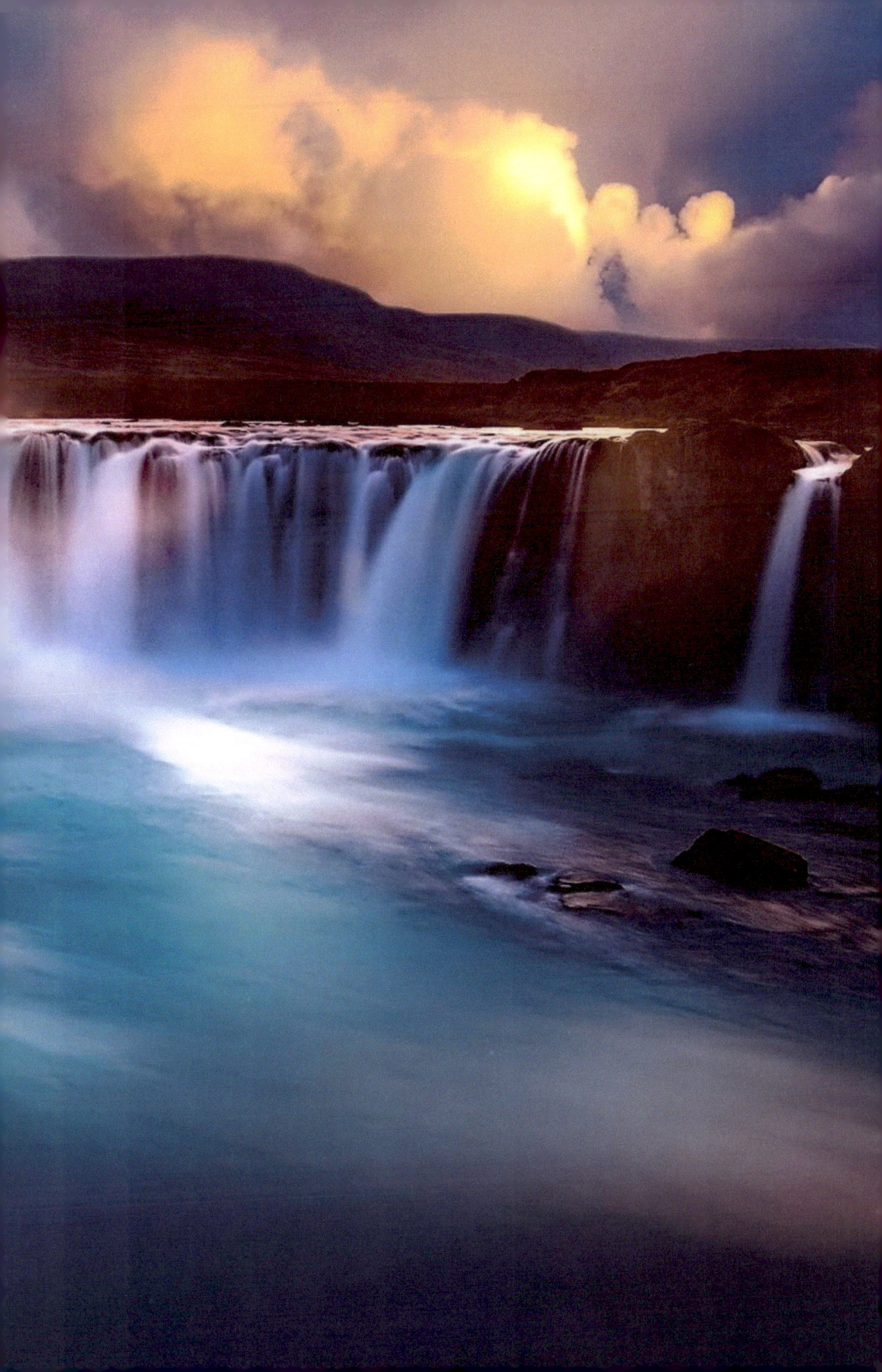

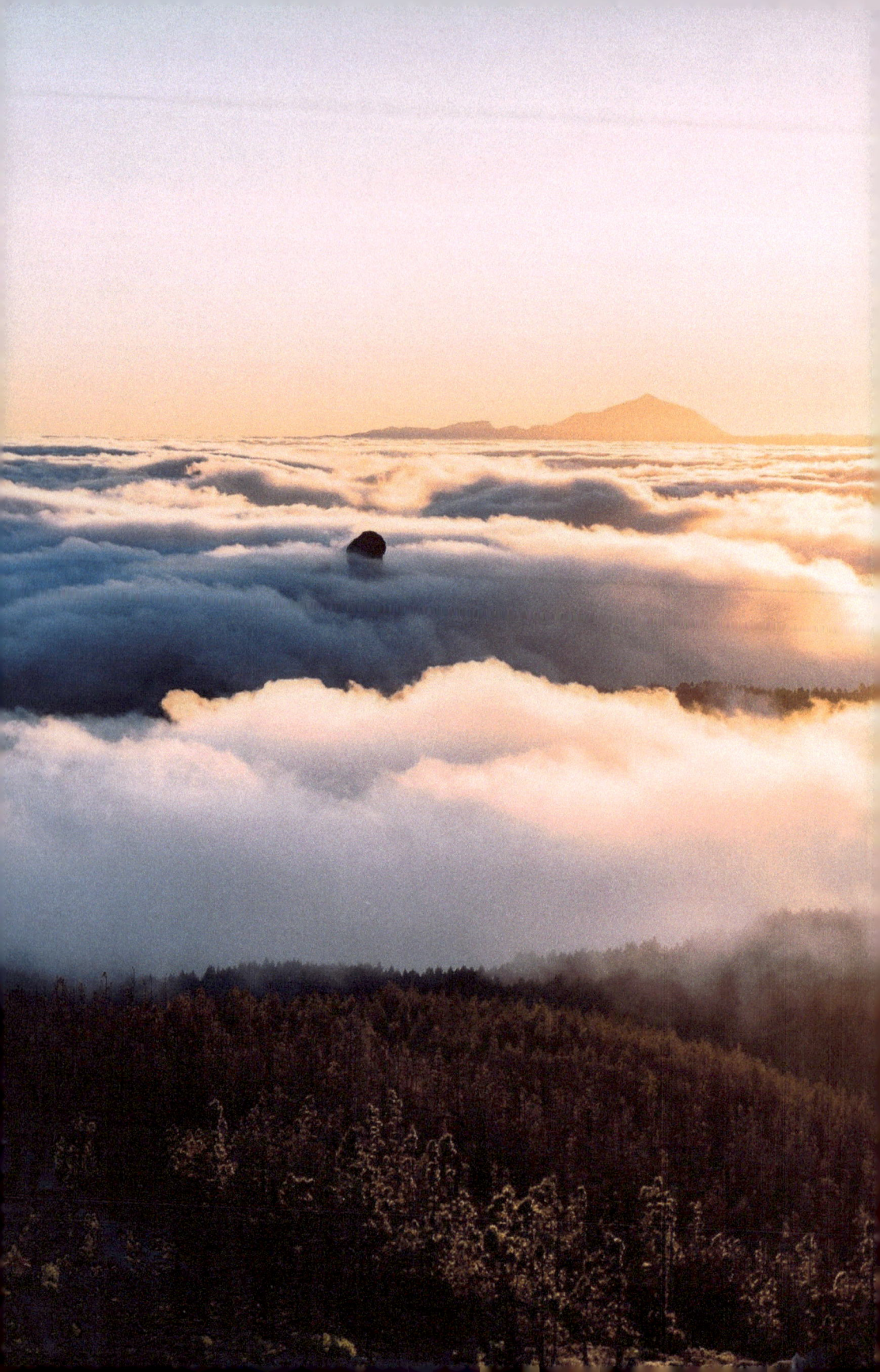

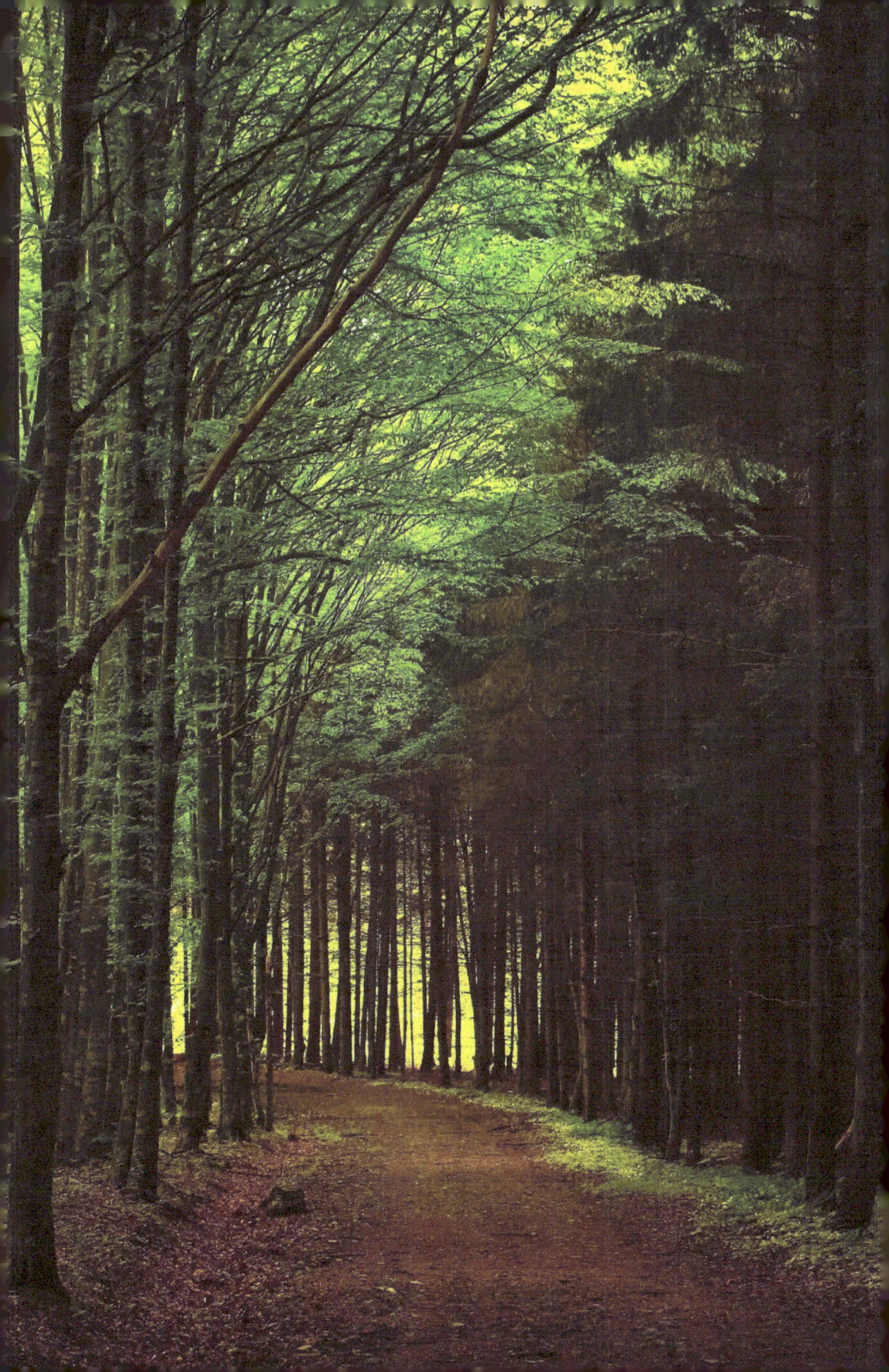

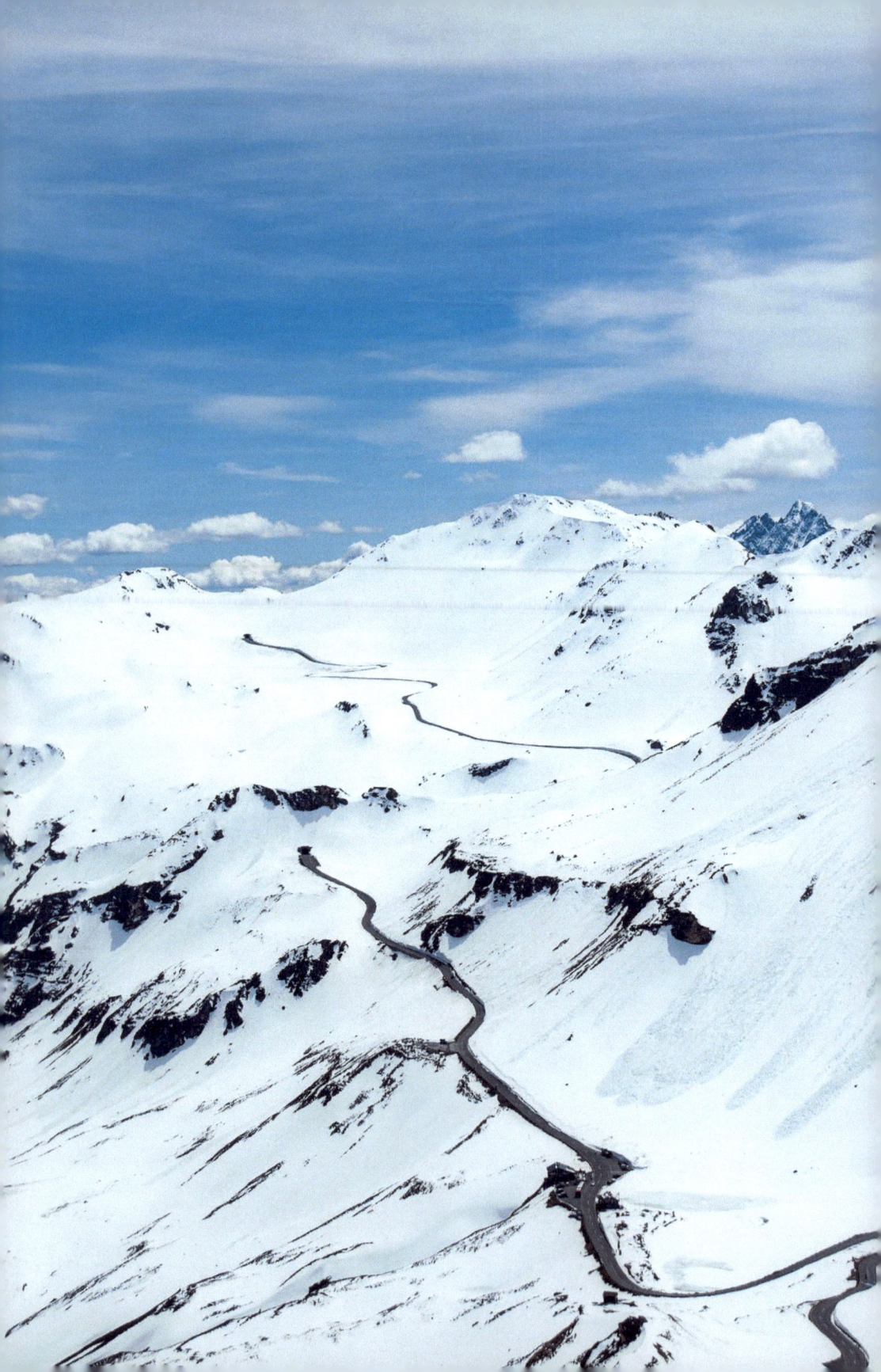

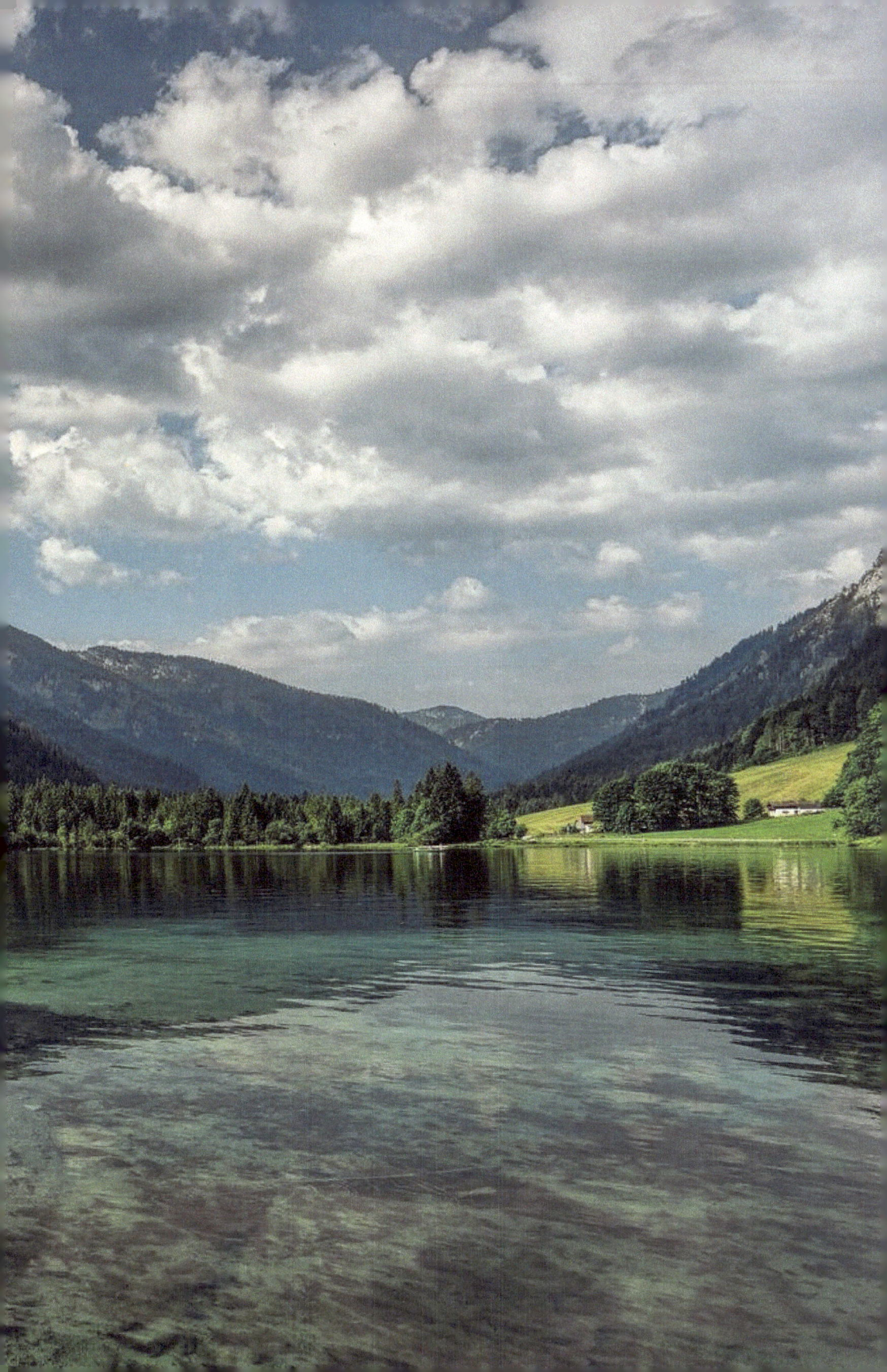

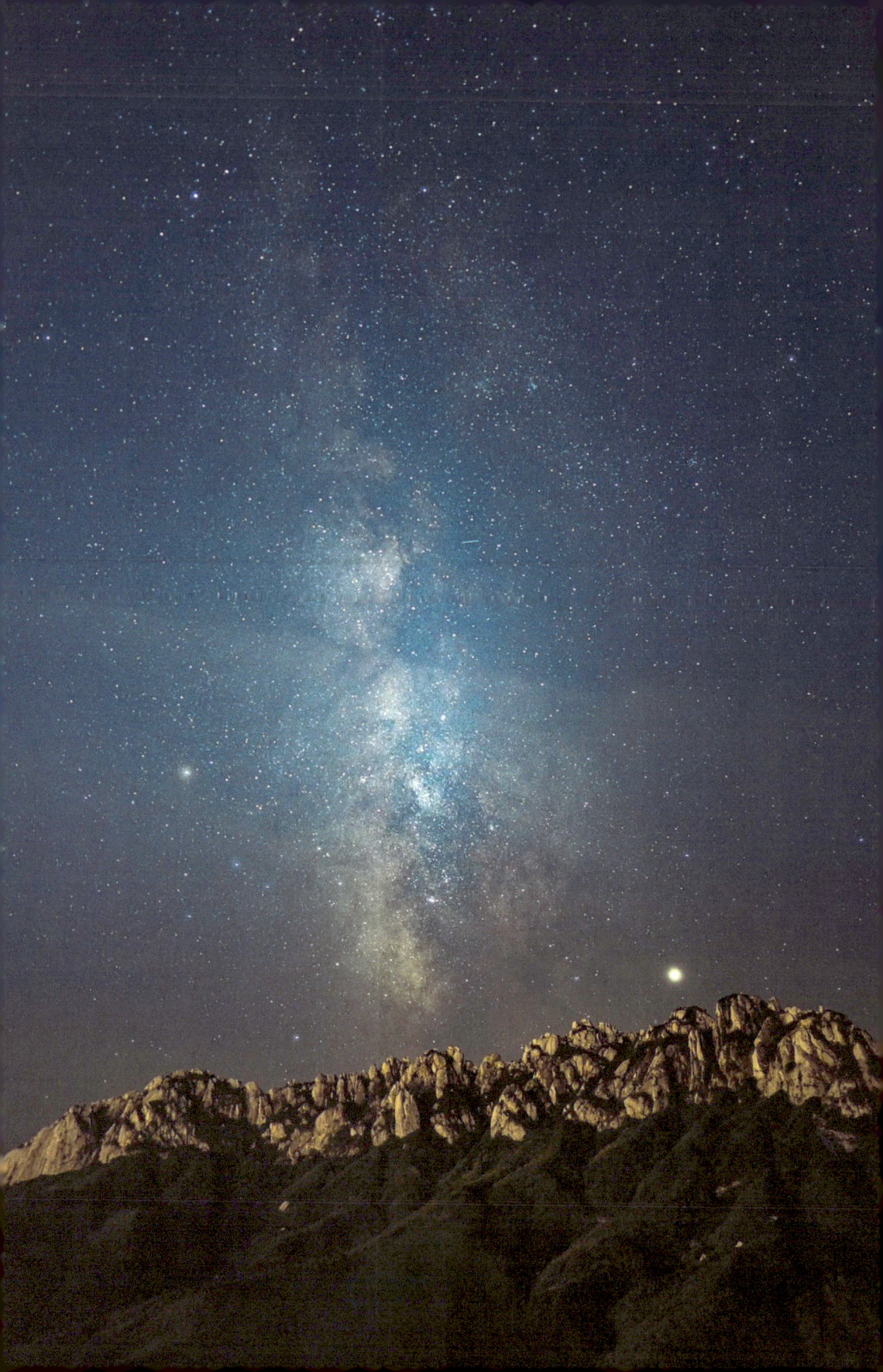

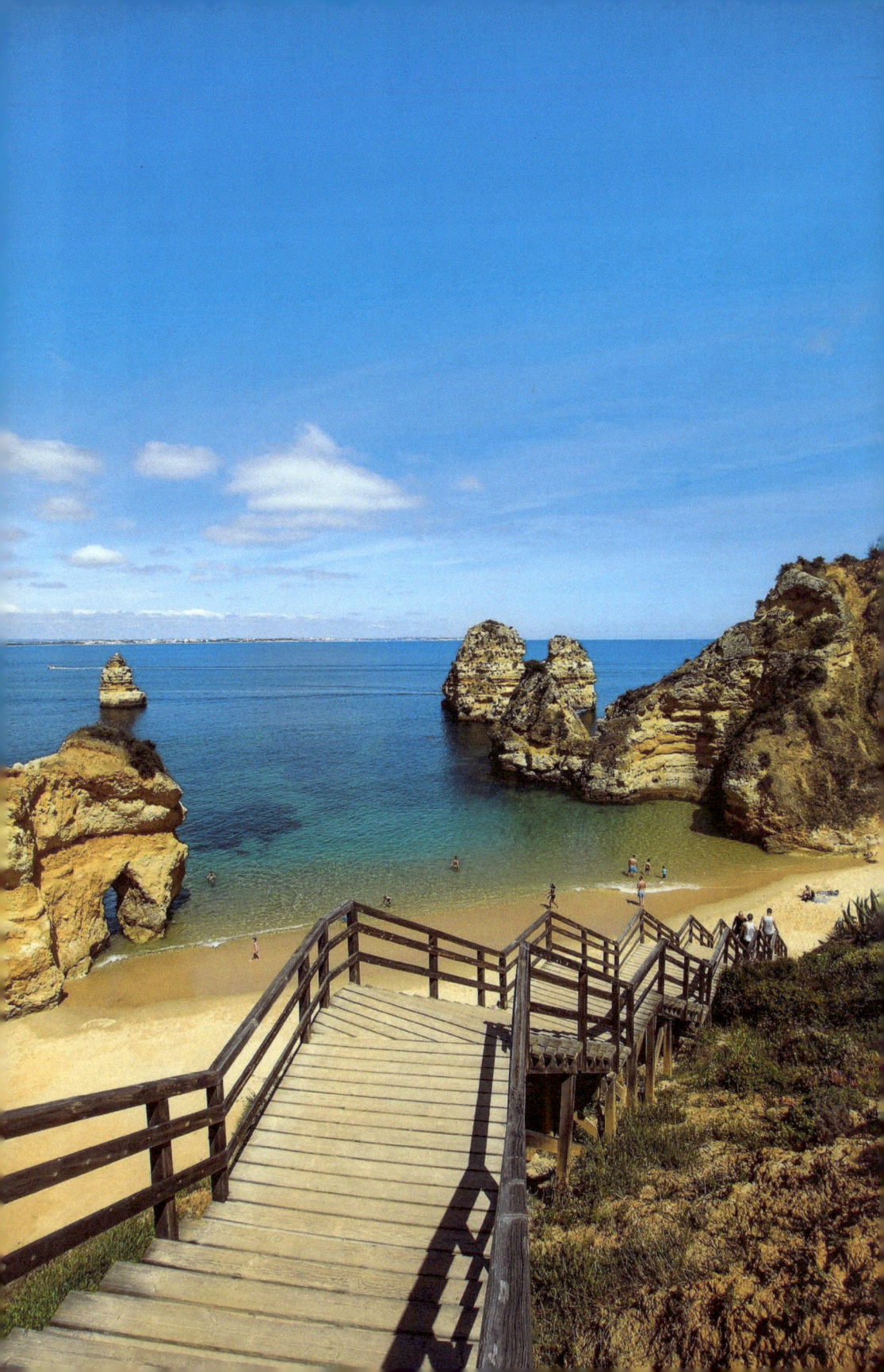

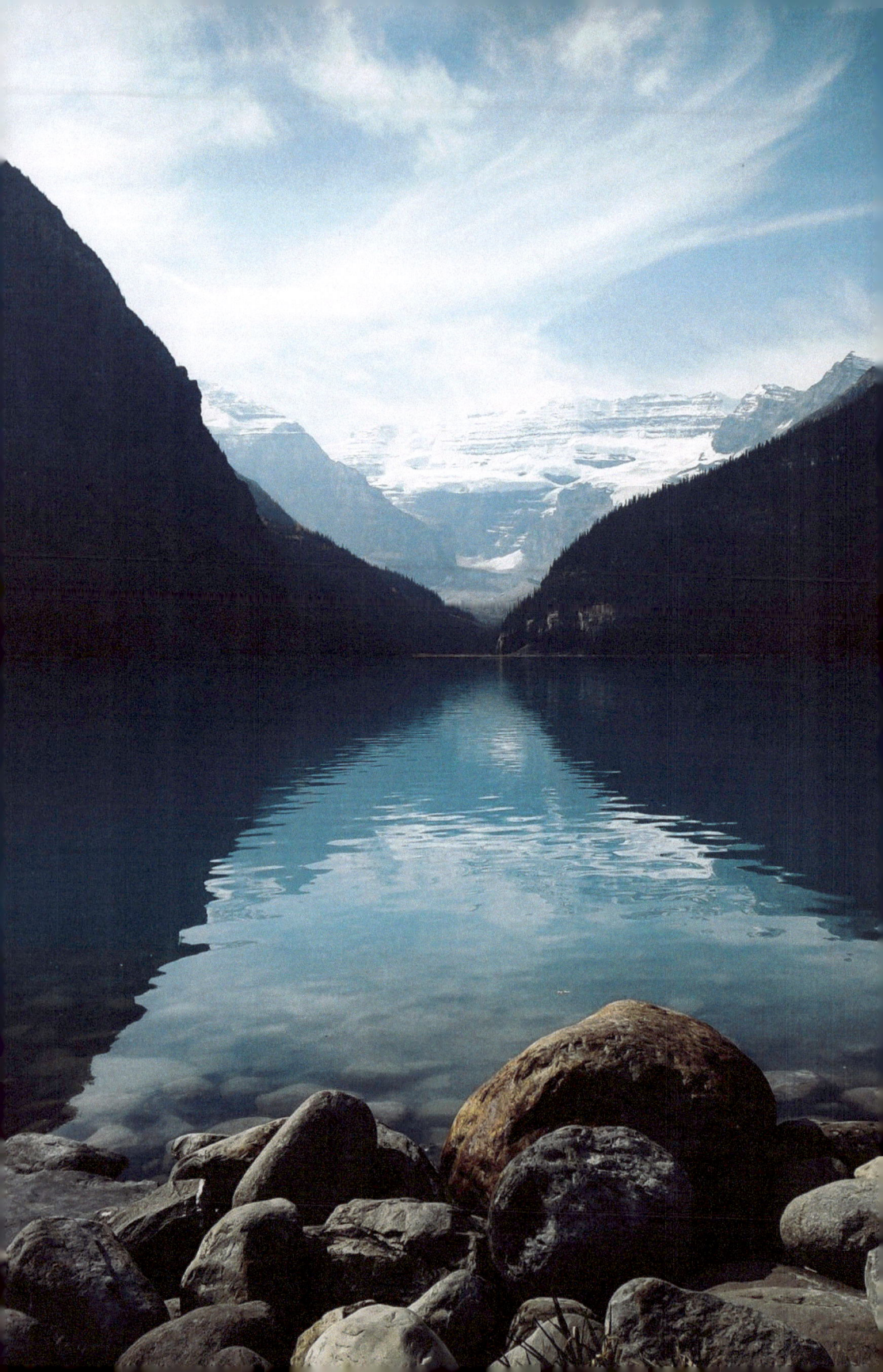

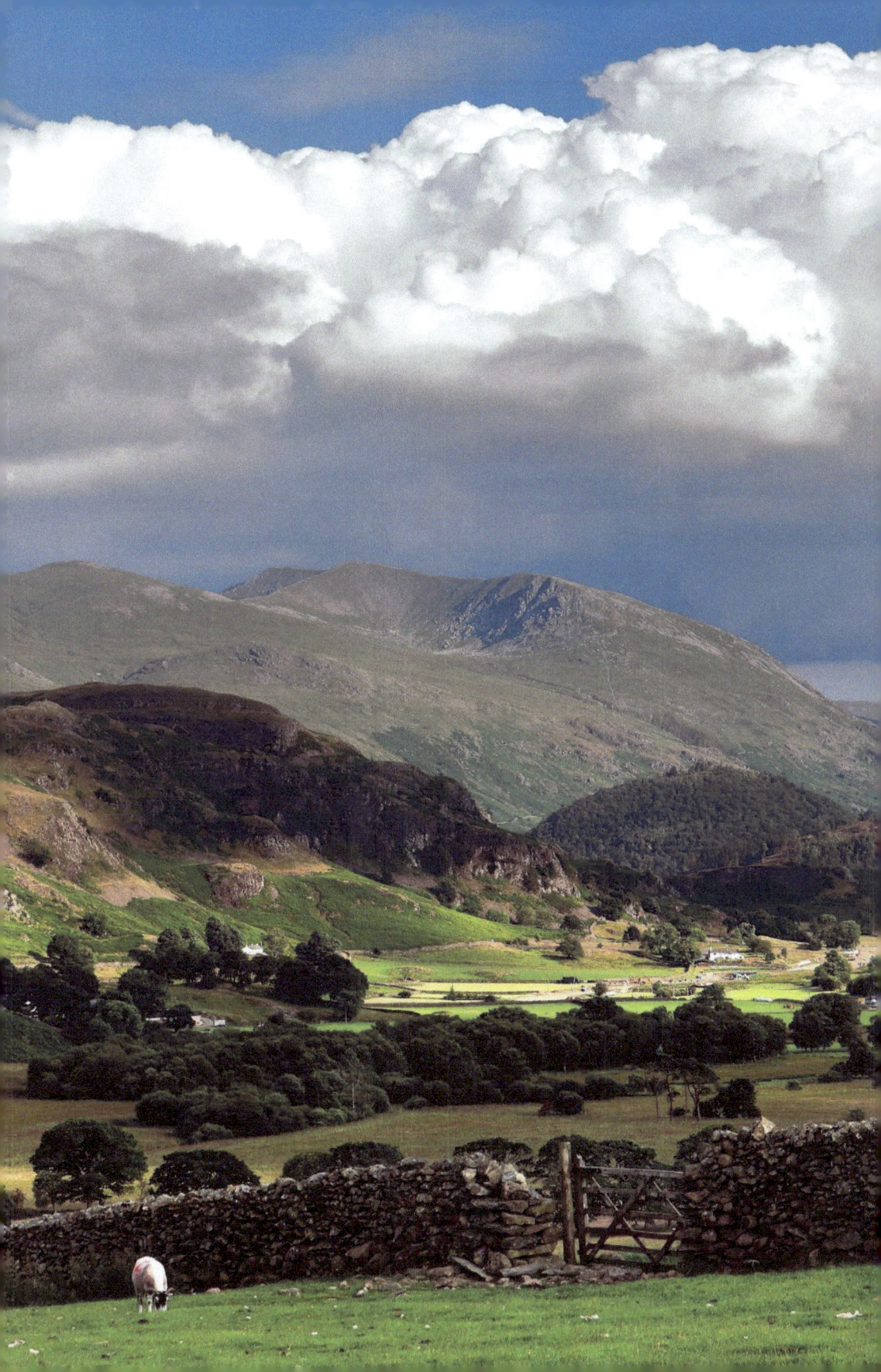

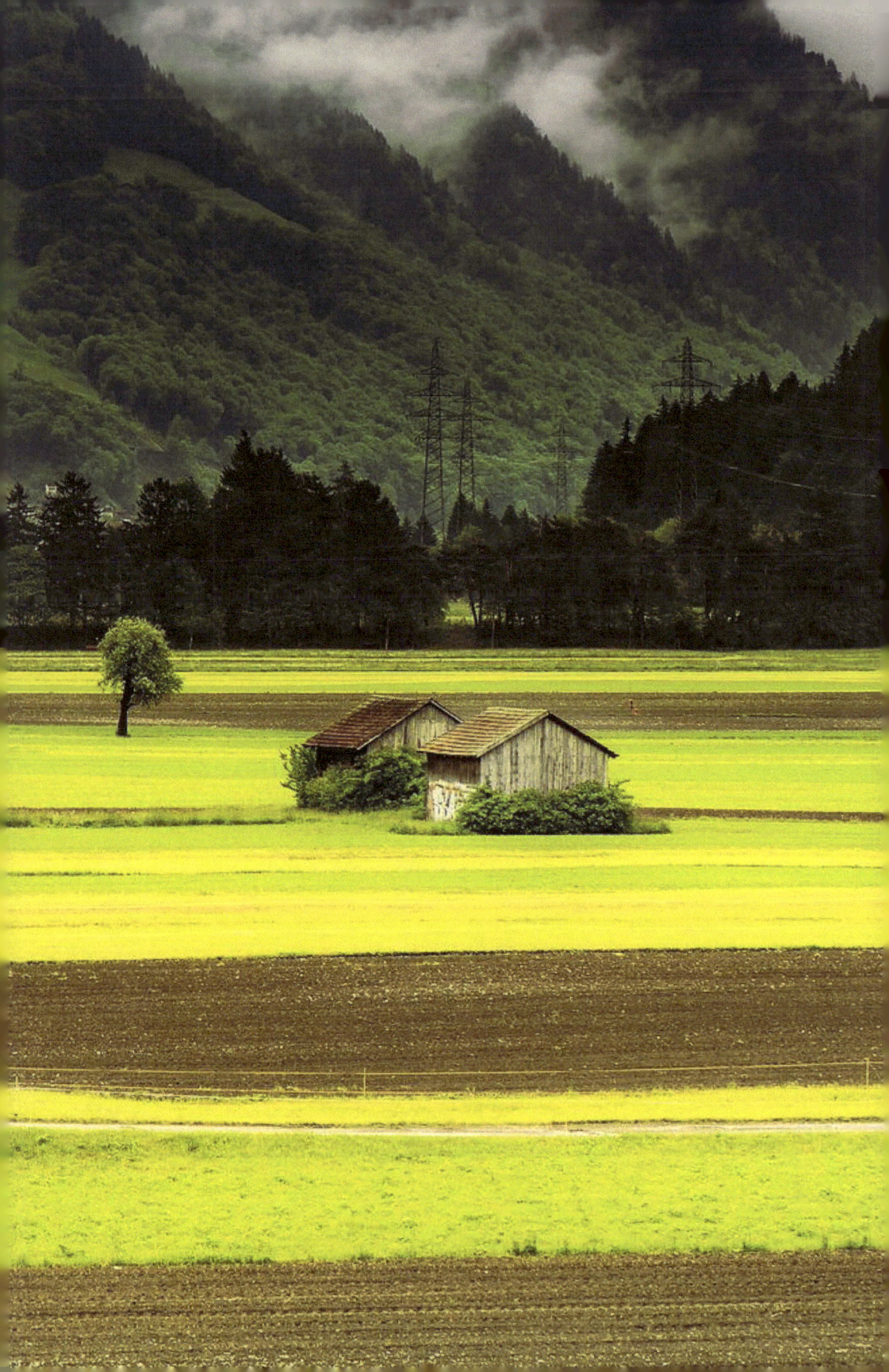

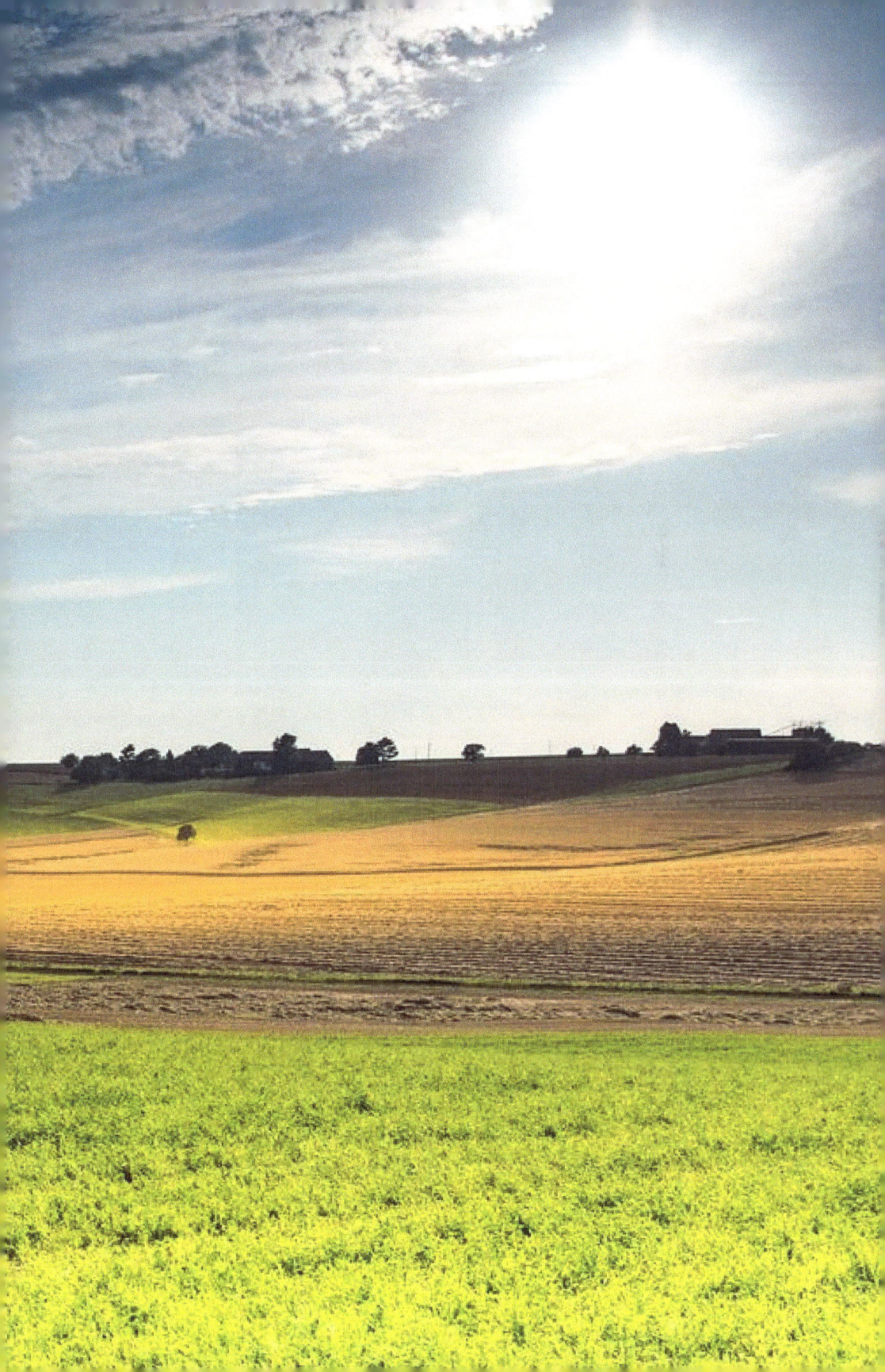

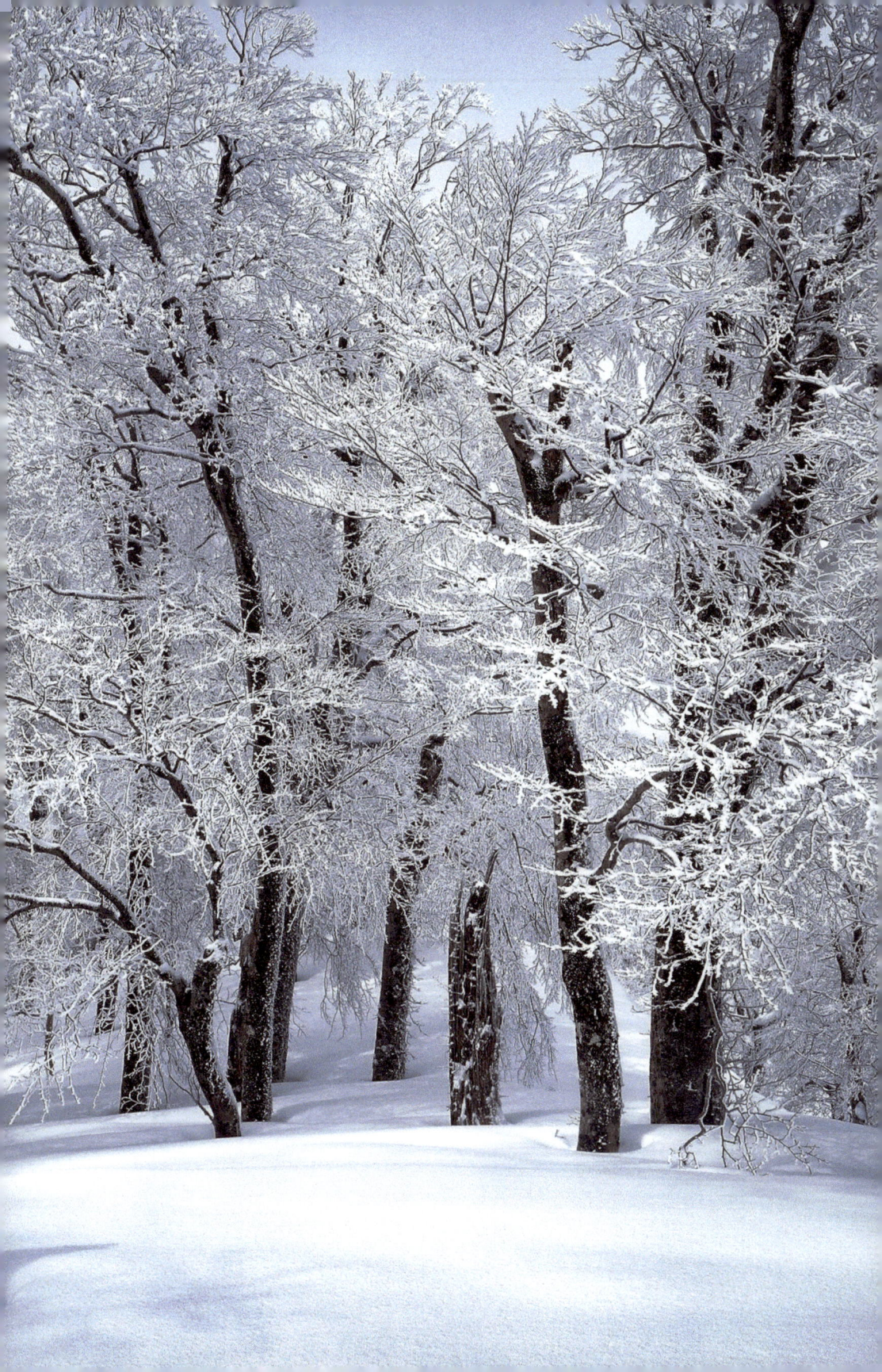

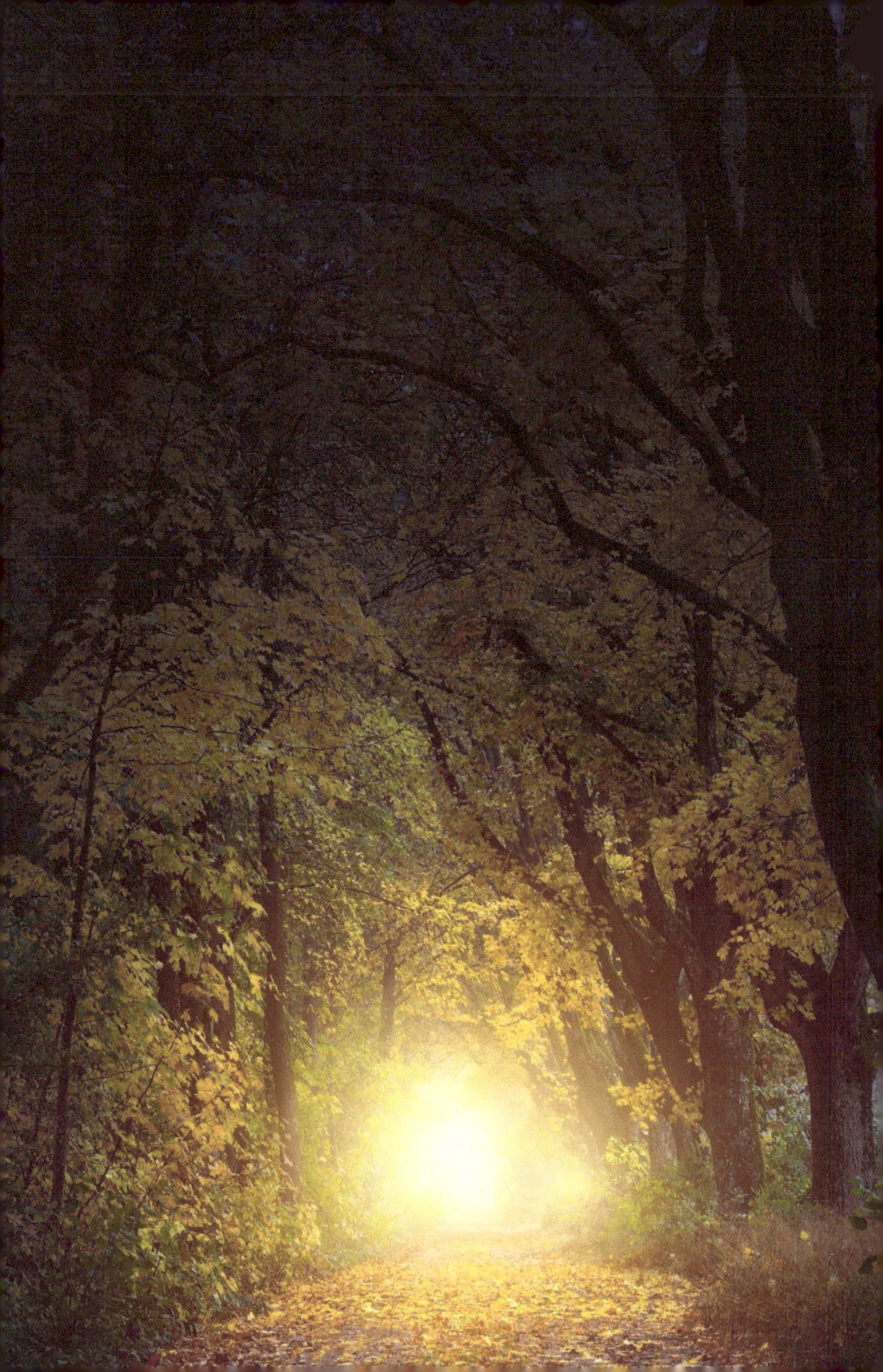

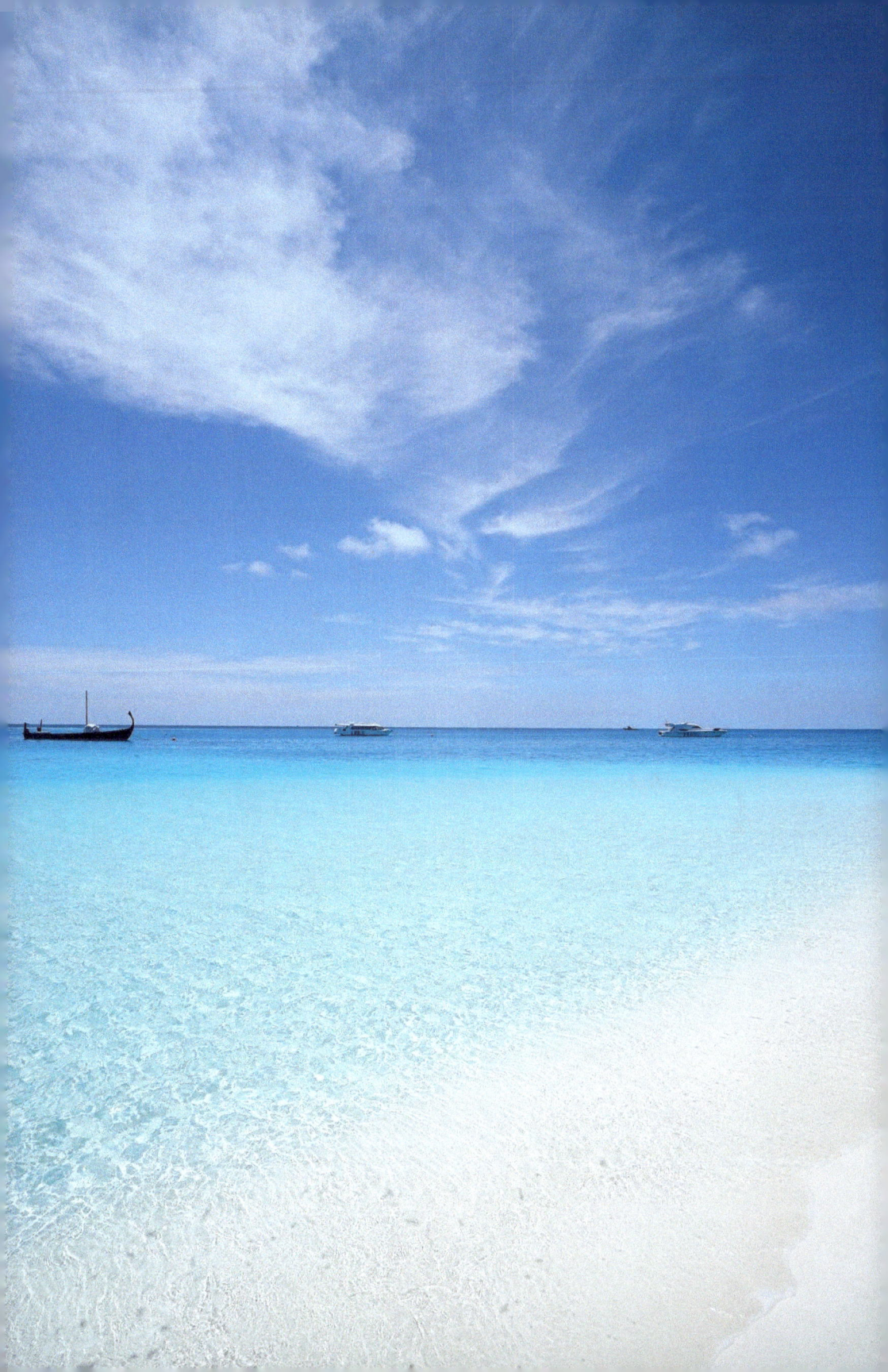

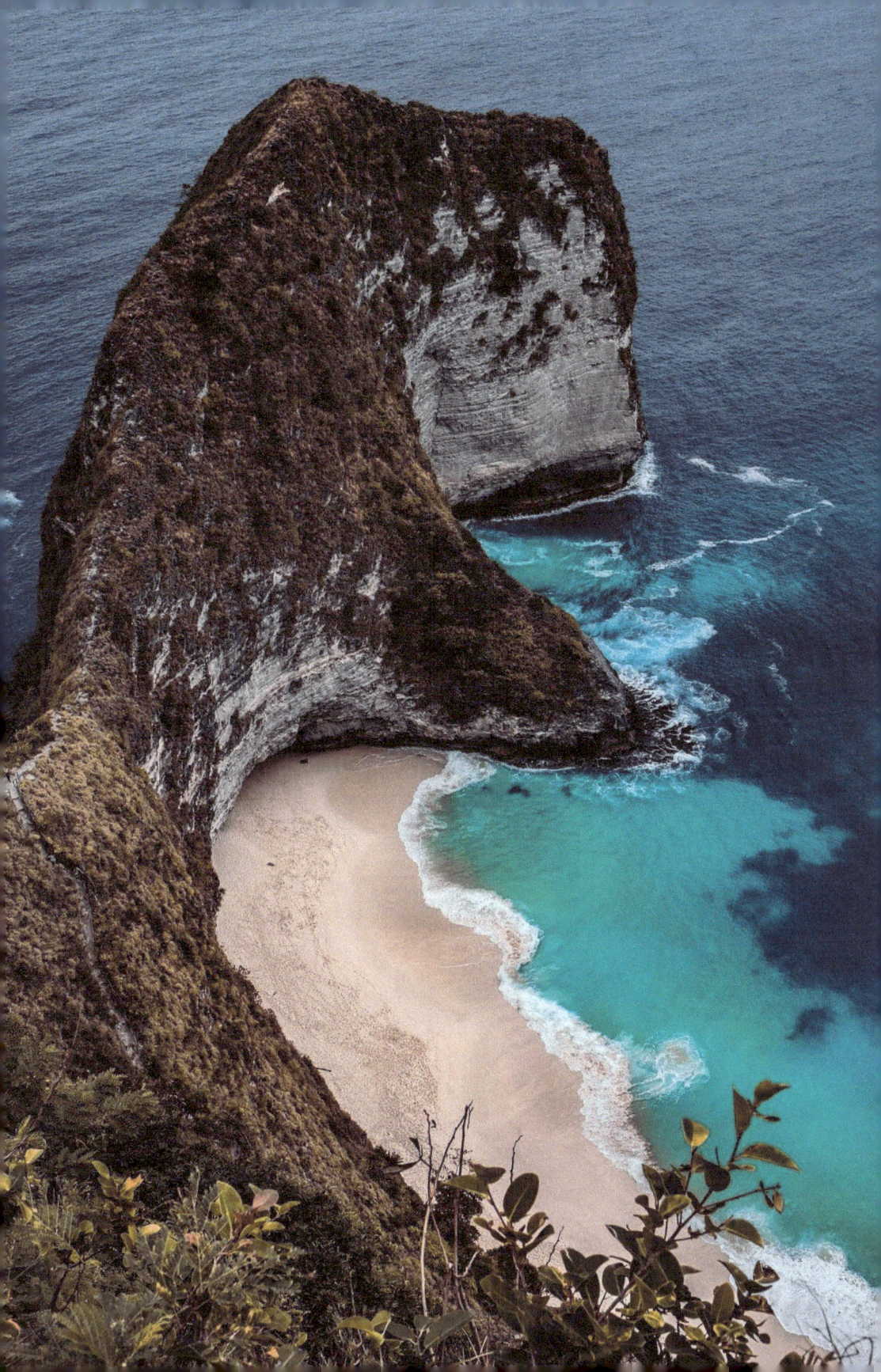

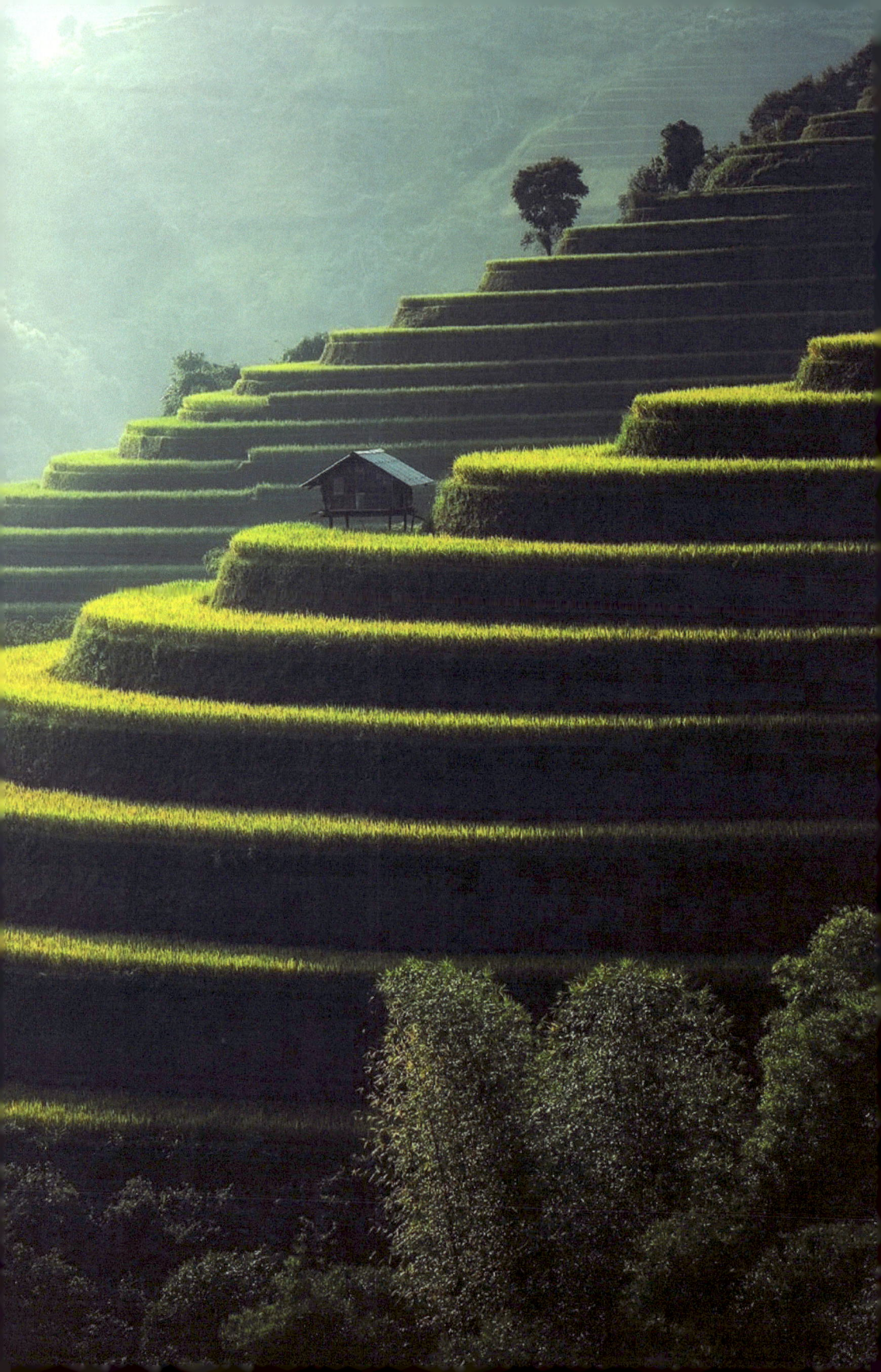

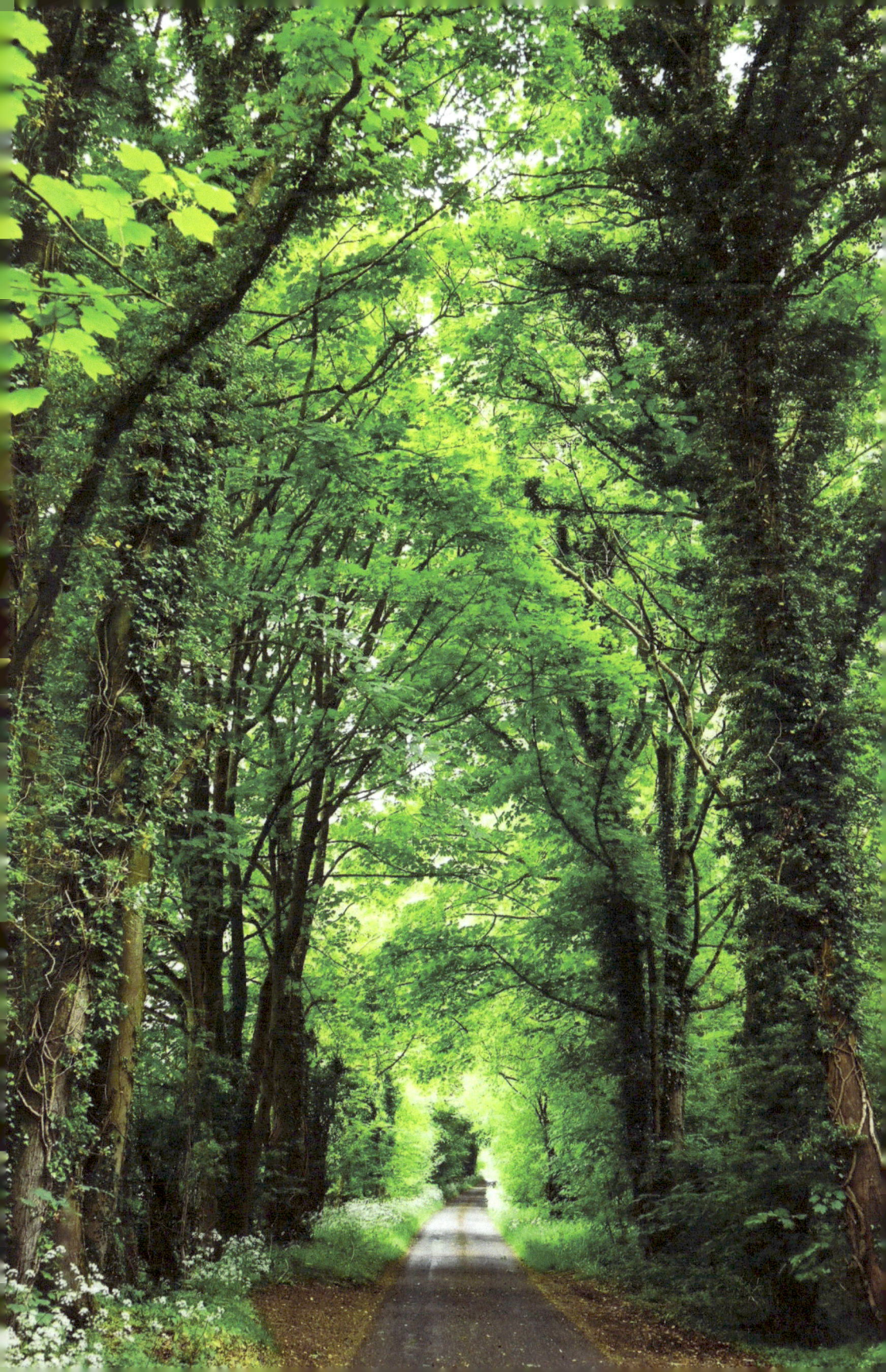

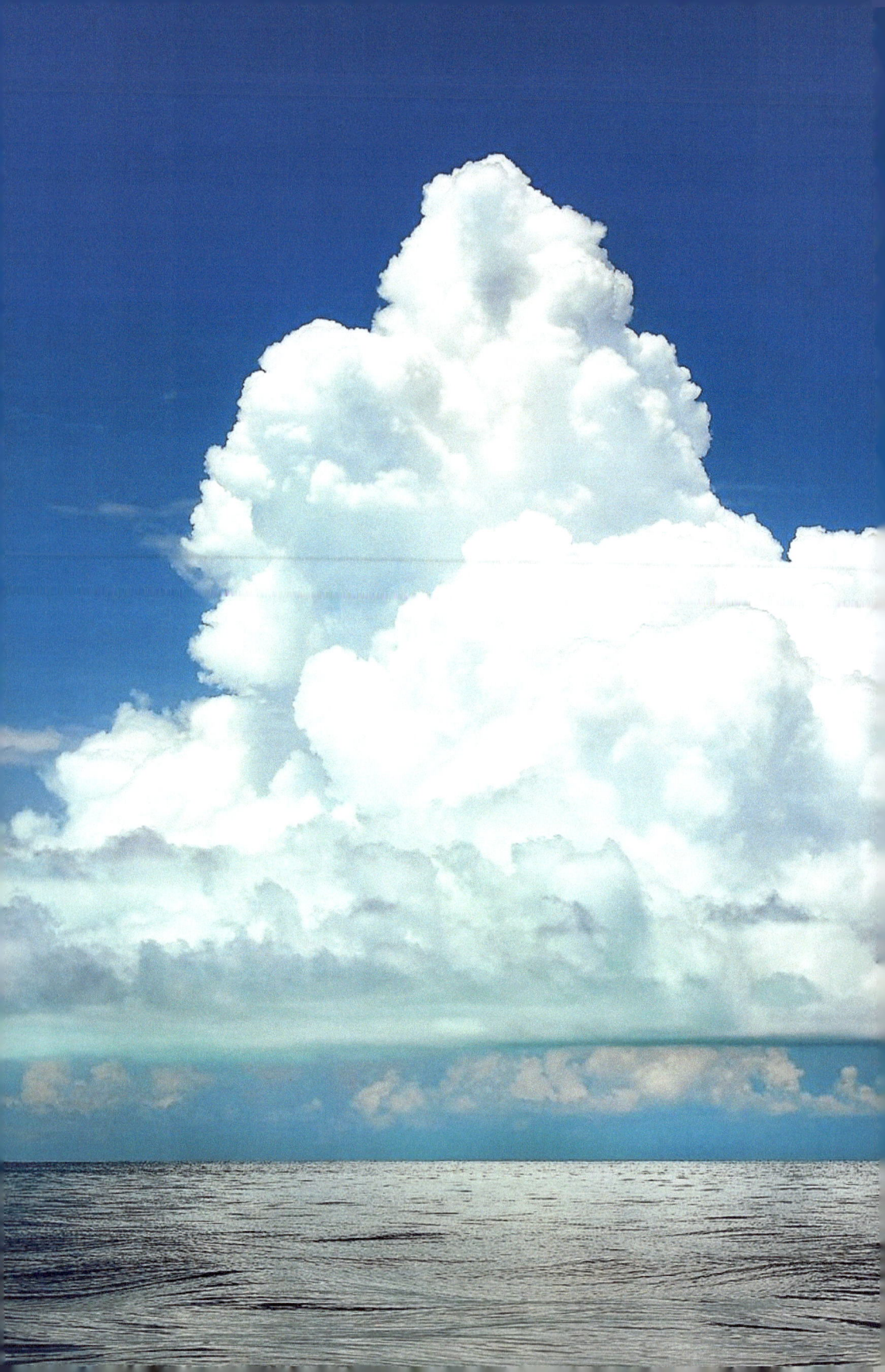

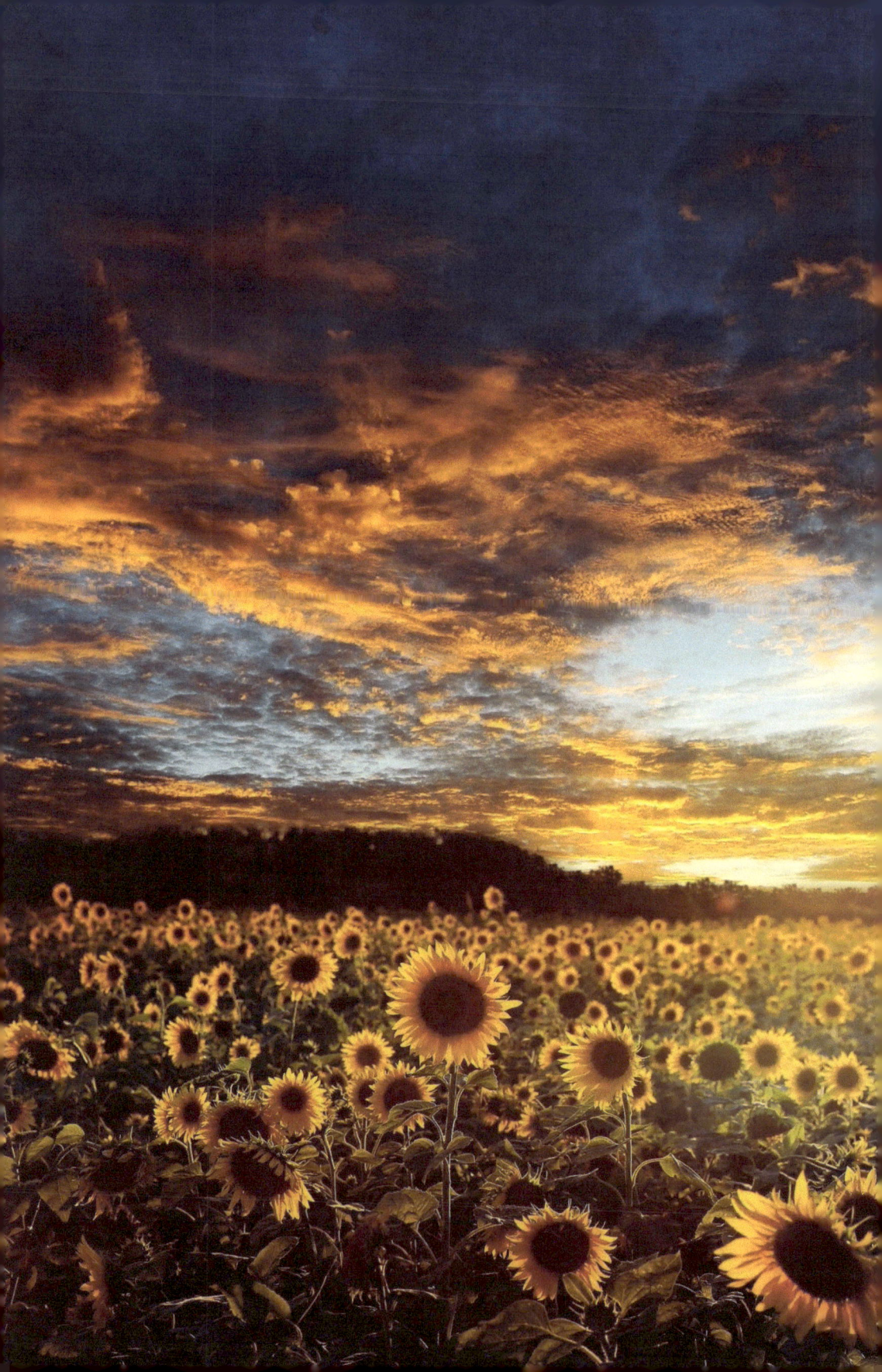

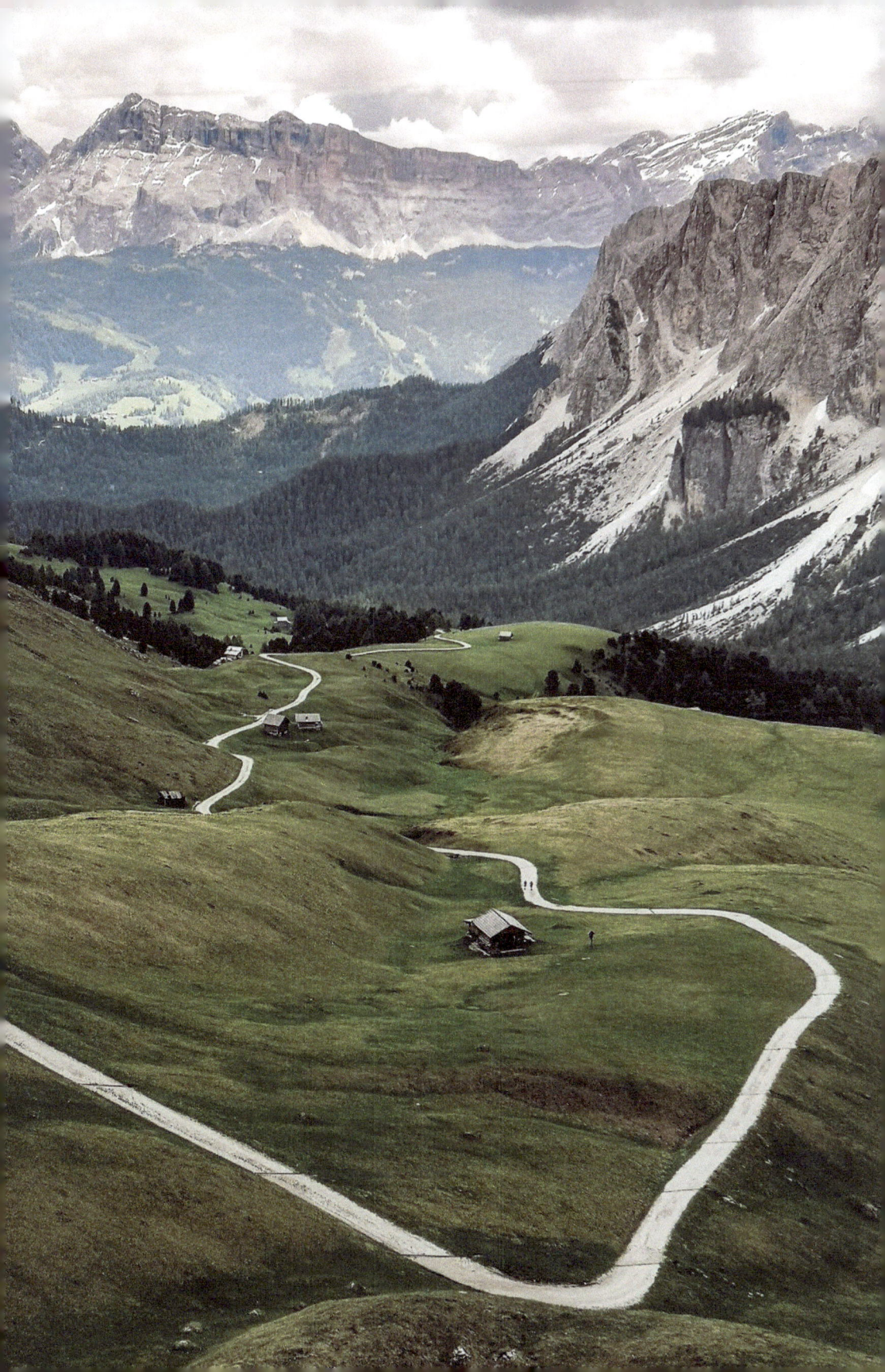

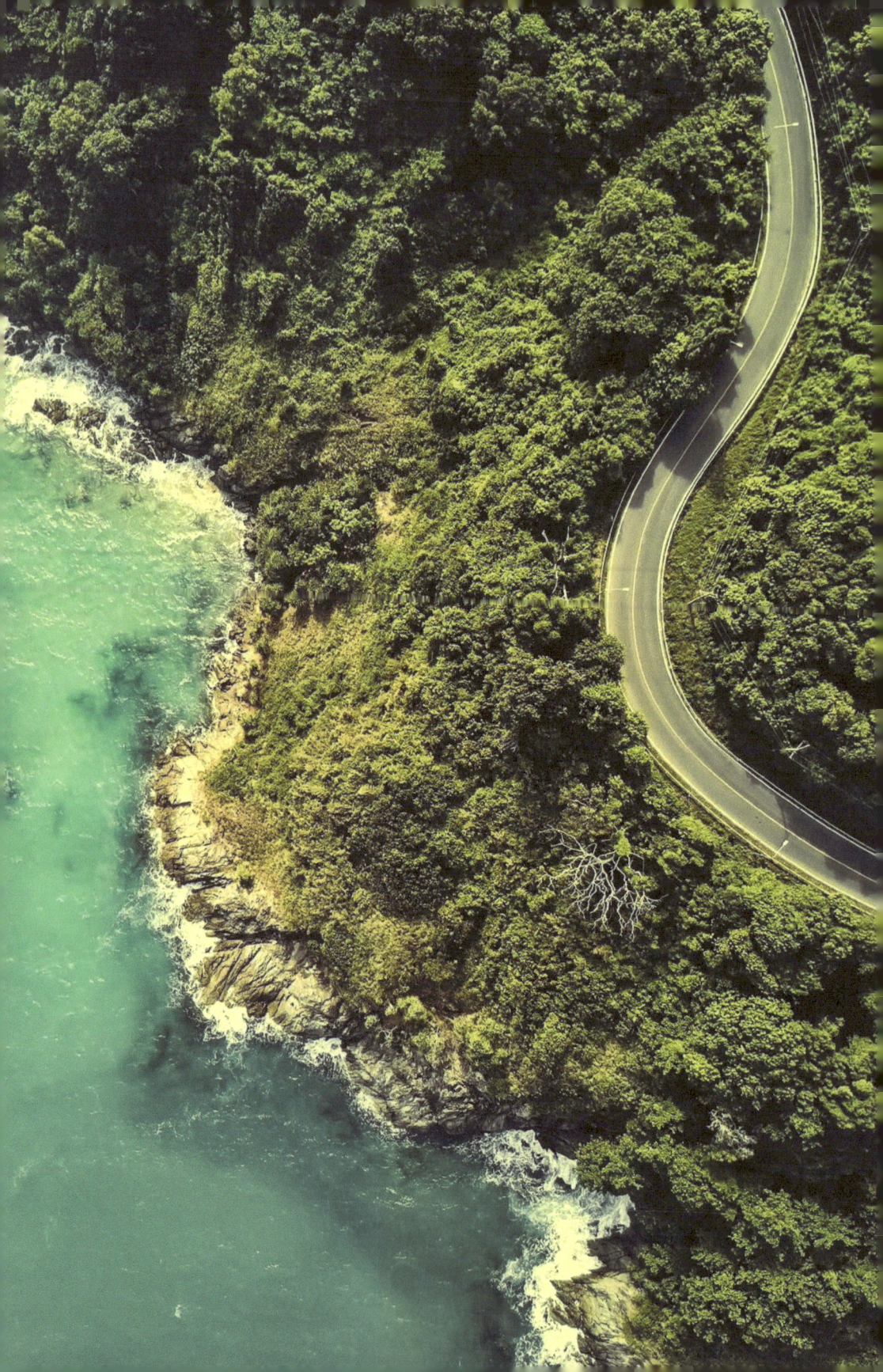

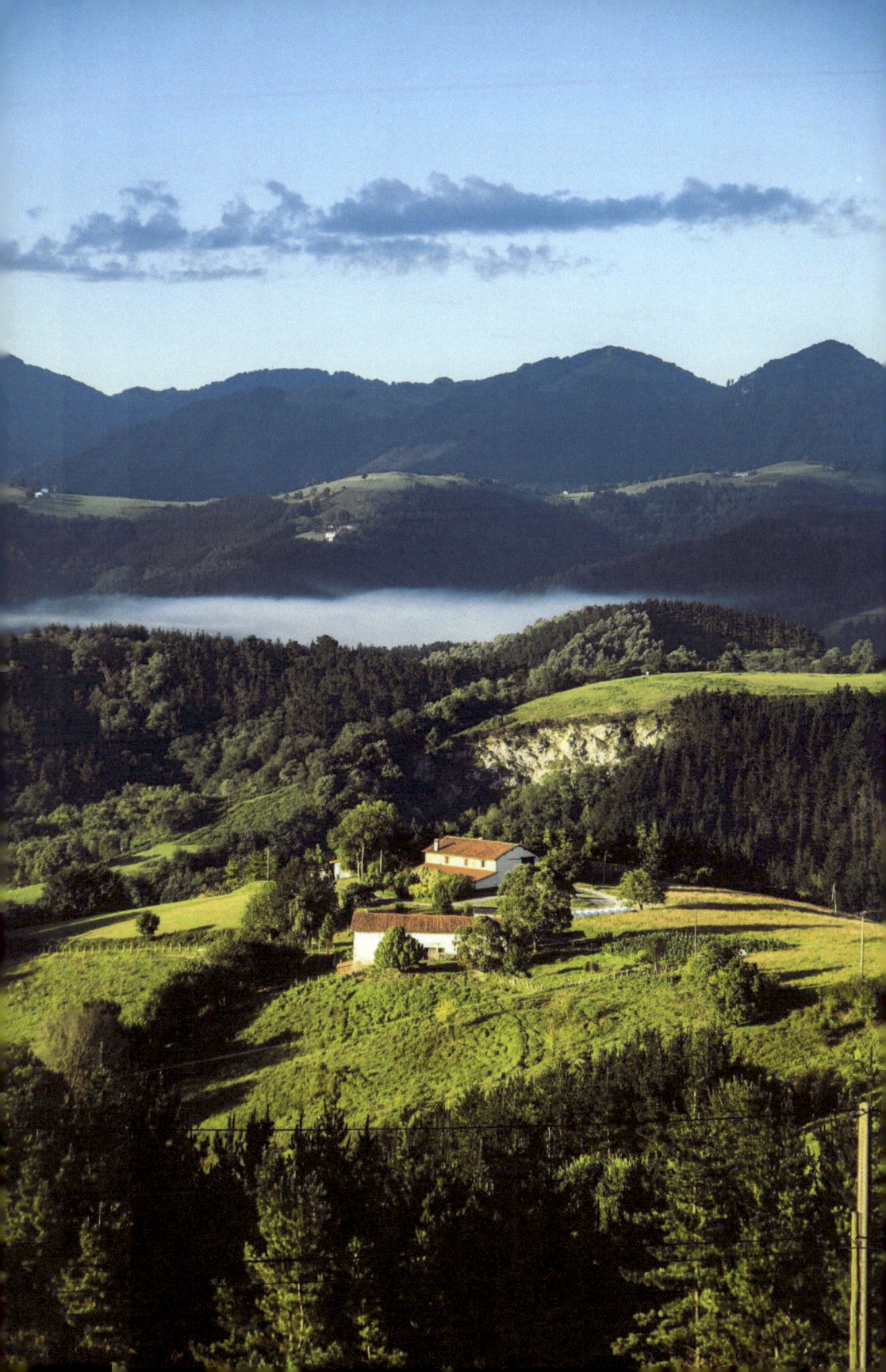

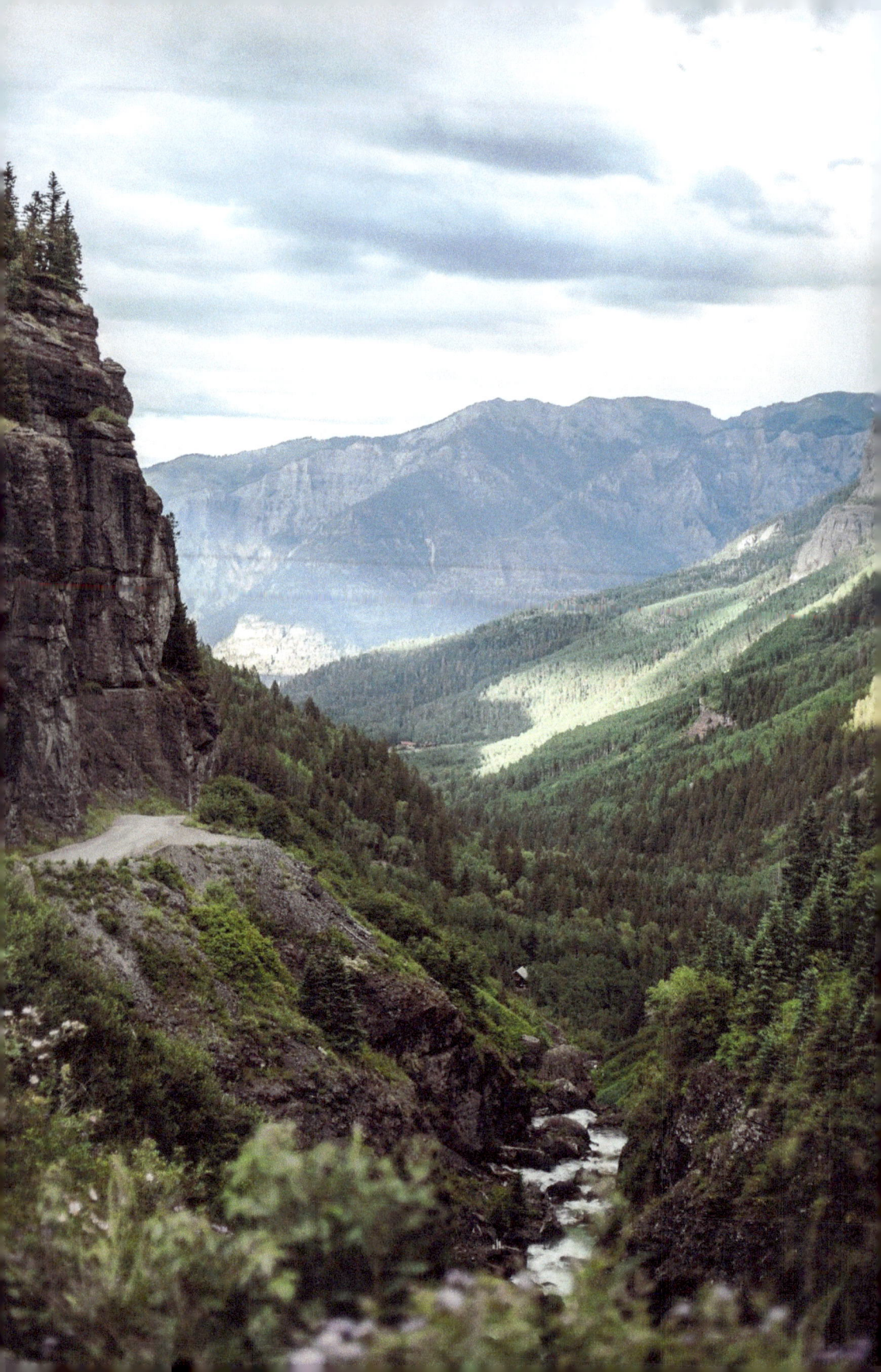

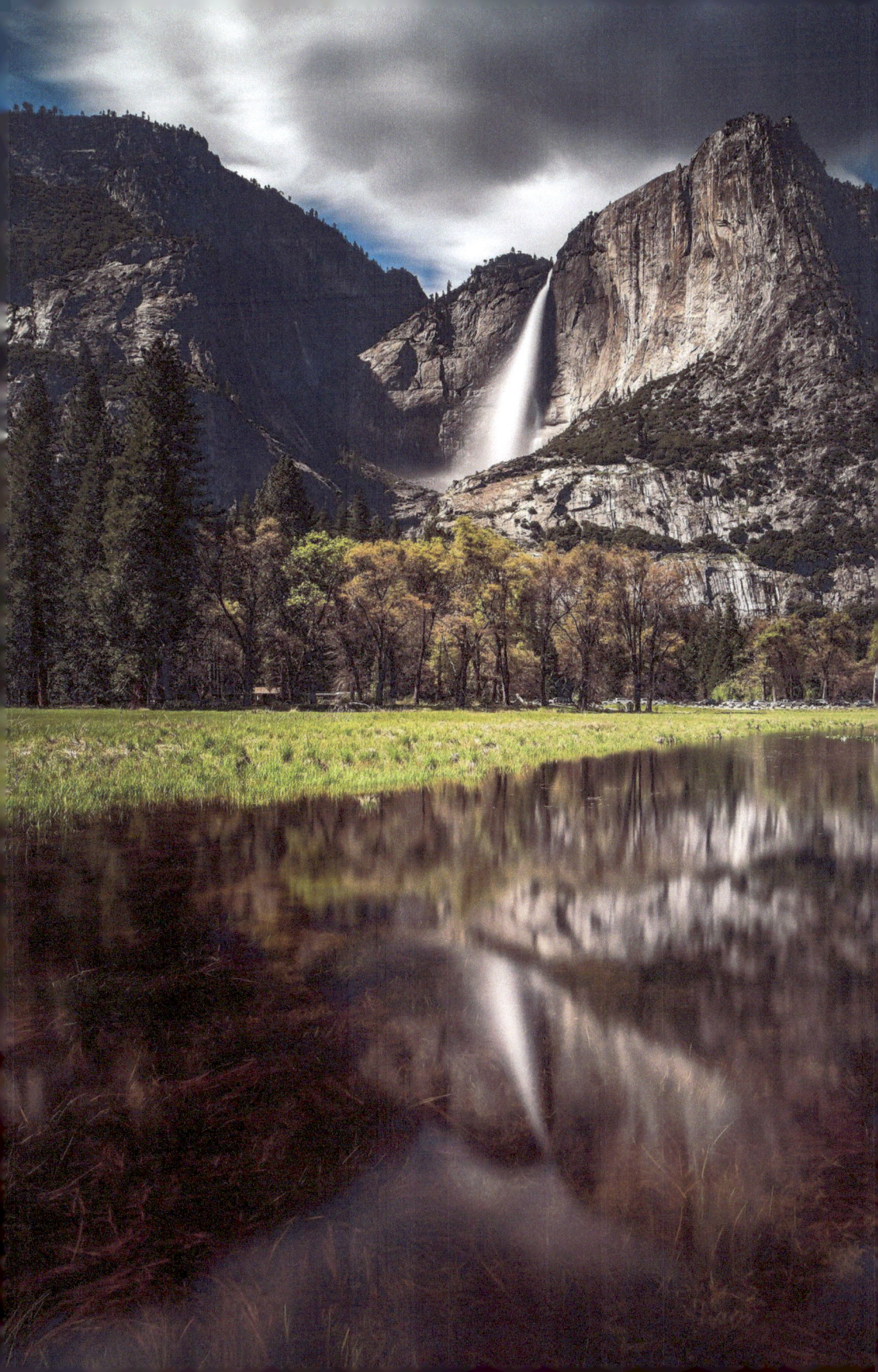

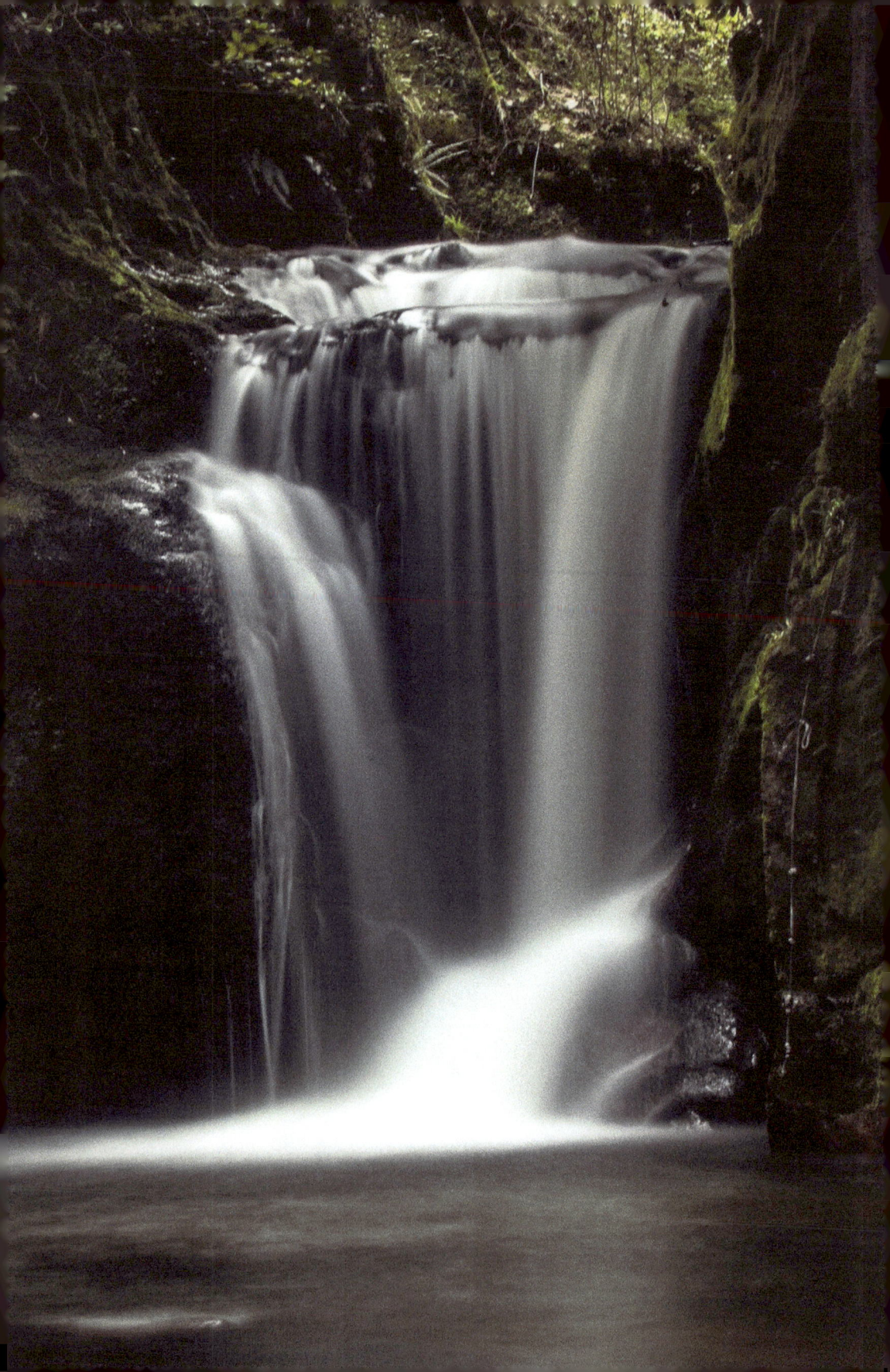

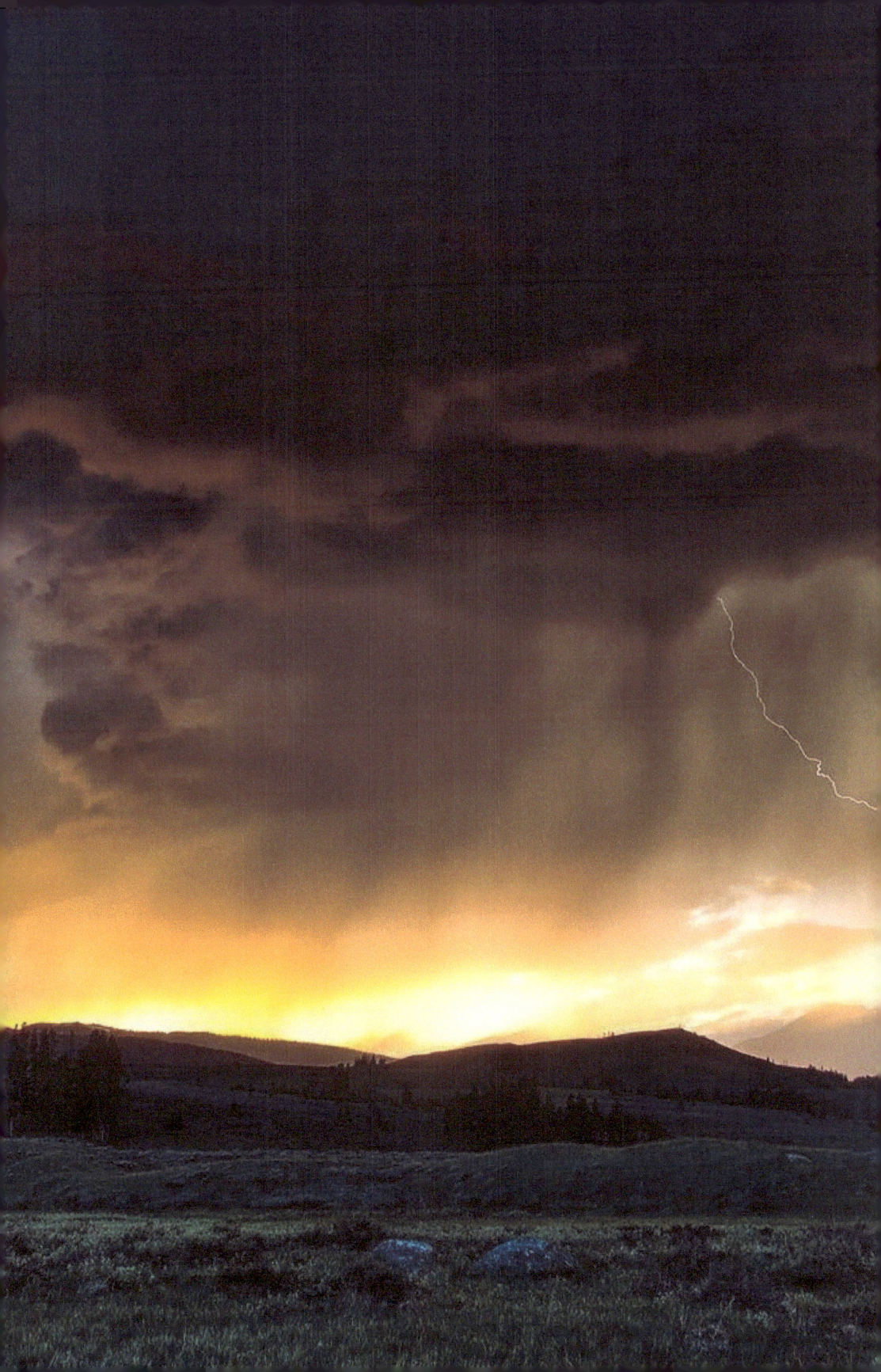

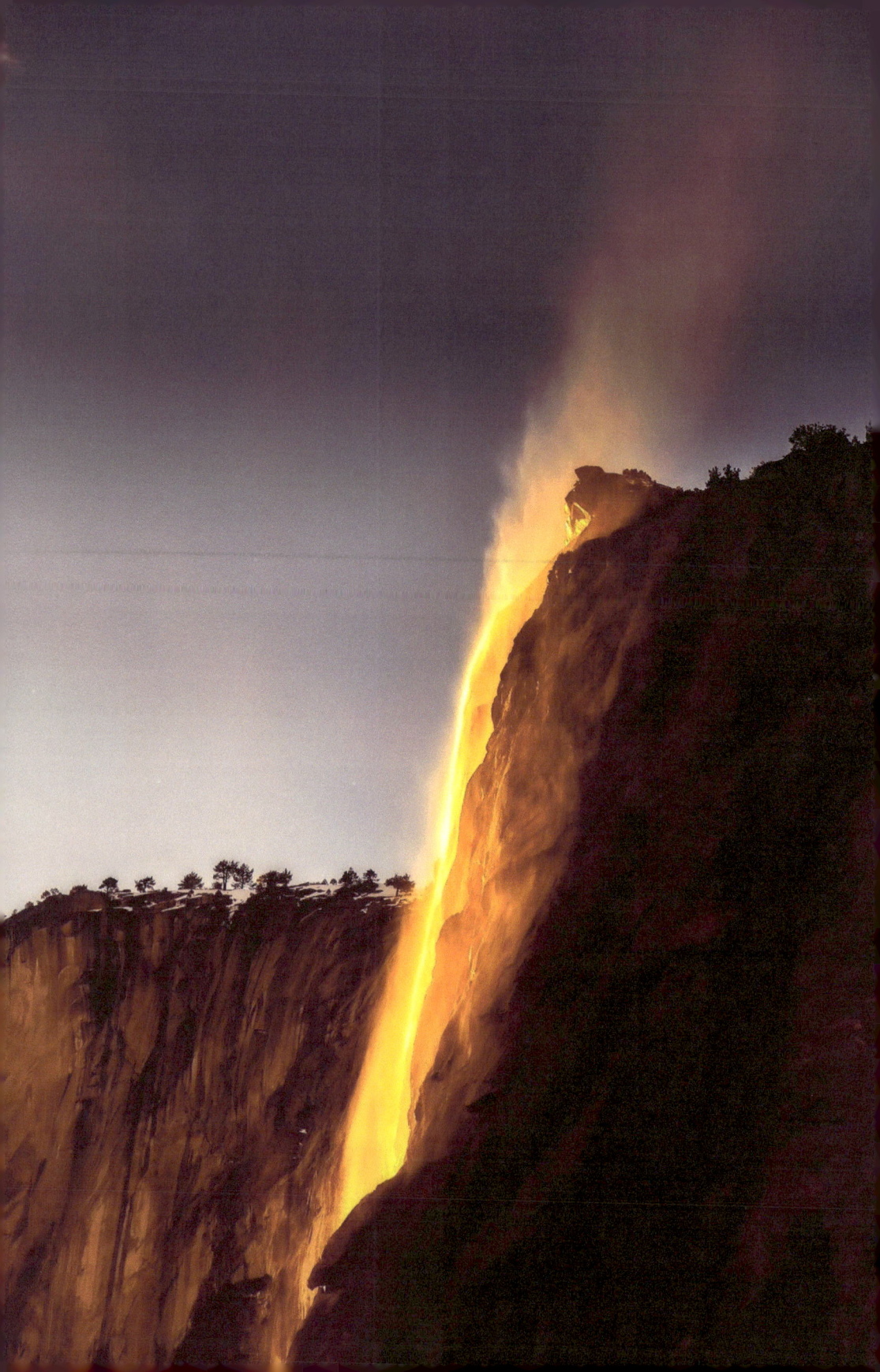

www.ingramcontent.com/pod-product-compliance
Lightning Source LLC
Chambersburg PA
CBHW040252220526
45473CB00001B/452